PAPER PLATES: WHEN PART OF YOUR FAMILY KEEPS KOSHER

edited by
Linda Loewenstein

A Jason Aronson Book

ROWMAN & LITTLEFIELD PUBLISHERS, INC.
Lanham • Boulder • New York • Toronto • Oxford

A JASON ARONSON BOOK

ROWMAN & LITTLEFIELD PUBLISHERS, INC.

Published in the United States of America
by Rowman & Littlefield Publishers, Inc.
A wholly owned subsidary of The Rowman & Littlefield Publishing Group, Inc.
4501 Forbes Boulevard, Suite 200, Lanham, Maryland 20706
www.rowmanlittlefield.com

PO Box 317
Oxford
OX2 9RU, UK

Copyright © 2003 by Linda Lowenstein
First Rowman & Littlefield edition 2004

British Library Cataloguing in Publication Information Available

Library of Congress Cataloging-in-Publication Data

Paper plates : when part of your family keeps kosher / [compiled] by Linda Lowenstein.
   p. cm.
  Includes index.
  ISBN 0-7657-6199-8 (pbk)
   1. Jewish families—Religious Life—United States. 2. Orthodox Judaism—
Relations—Nontraditional Jews. 3. Jews—Return to Orthodox Judaism. 4. Jews—
United States—Interviews. 5. Jews—Dietary Laws. 6. Judaism—United States—
Customs and practices. I. Lowenstein, Linda.
BM723.P366 2003
296.7'4—dc21   200346254

Printed in the United States of America

♾™ The paper used in this publication meets the minimum requirements of American
National Standard for Information Sciences—Permanence of Paper for Printed Library
Materials, ANSI/NISO Z39.48-1992.

*To my parents
with love*

CONTENTS

Part IV: Conclusion

NOT Ⓤ

Many of the participants in this book describe their dietary practices. Readers should not necessarily assume that these practices meet all standards of *kashruth*. In other words, ask your rabbi.

ACKNOWLEDGMENTS

I am indebted to those contributors who generously allowed me into their kitchens (kosher and non-kosher) and shared their most private feelings about religious observance and their families. This book is theirs.

There are a number of people who read parts of the manuscript early on and whose good counsel and enthusiasm were invaluable. Those friends include Charlotte Smokler, Laurie Travers, Karen Mitchell, Galina Norkin, Bonnie and Herb Horn, Rachel Stein, Susan Cohen, and Kathy Kaiser. I owe a special debt to wordsmith Alice Levine, for her talent and friendship.

In addition to the contributors whose names appear on the essays or interviews, there were many people with whom I talked at length, people whose general perspectives helped shape this book. I am very grateful to Rabbi Daniel Goldberger, Marilyn Scheinfeldt, the Guth family, the Wolfe family, the Leventhal family, Leo Katz, Nama Frenkel, Sandy Kozinn, David Zoller, Harry Nachman, and Lisa and Jerry Japha.

And, finally, I must somehow find the words to thank my family. Without my brother, Michael, this book truly would not have happened. My daughter Johanna, now an adult and a journalism student, was always willing to "just look this over." My son, Avi's skepticism about this project kept me going. My daughter, Talia asked only that I dedicate the book to her, but she understood when I didn't. And, finally, thank you to my husband, Mark, the most patient man in the world. I love you all.

INTRODUCTION

*D*uring World War II, while the Jewish people were being systematically slaughtered in Europe, my father was playing Ping-Pong. He was an American G.I. stationed in Europe, and he entertained our troops by playing exhibition Ping-Pong in Mickey Rooney's Jeep show.

As a child, I loved looking at pictures of the war. "Look, there's Daddy and that movie star," we'd exclaim. We knew absolutely nothing about the Holocaust.

Our home was ethnically Jewish but totally non-observant. By totally non-observant, I mean the we-had-a-Christmas-tree type of home. All four of my grandparents had been born in the United States so we never heard Yiddish, never ate rugelach. We ate Oreos, which were then made with lard. Yet, my father's partners were Jewish, almost all my parents' friends were Jewish, we lived in a Jewish neighborhood, and my mother always asked the last name of my date.

My two younger brothers and I went to Sunday school but no one had a bar or bat mitzvah. We were confirmed. Just before my confirmation service at Temple Emanuel in Chicago, I had an individual, private meeting with Rabbi Herman Schaalman, a wonderful man. He asked me my Hebrew name. I didn't have a Hebrew name, but I was too embarrassed to tell him so I mumbled, "Leah." It's been my Hebrew name ever since. I don't know what happens if, in a synagogue, you lie to a rabbi about your Hebrew name, but I've always been a little worried about it.

When my youngest brother, Michael, was a senior at Wesleyan University, he was accepted to Harvard Law School. For my parents, my mother especially, this was the ultimate achievement. But Michael decided to give up Harvard and go to Israel to study. This young man, who didn't know an *aleph* from a *bet*, was, in my mother's mind, throwing away his future.

Michael had been in Israel for about three years, becoming more and more observant, when my brother Larry announced that he was engaged to marry a lovely British girl named Lynda, a non-Jew. Although neither bride nor groom was interested in keeping a Jewish home, my parents hired a rabbi to conduct the service. My brother Michael refused to return to the United States for the wedding.

At that point, something inside my mother died. She said, "If this is what Judaism is, if this is what it does to families, if it means that you cannot take joy in your brother's happiness, then I want nothing to do with it." She meant it.

Fast forward fifteen years.

Michael returned to the United States and earned an MBA from Northwestern University. In career terms, he has succeeded beyond my mother's wildest Harvard dreams. He's modern Orthodox, married to an FFB (*frum from birth*) young woman originally from Minneapolis, and they have four beautiful children. They live about twenty minutes away from my parents.

My mother does not own one kosher utensil.

For fifteen years, I have watched and whined about the tension in my family. So finally, I decided to whine out loud. I wanted to know how other families deal with the problems, what compromises people make, why keeping kosher isn't only about food but about identity and power struggles and values.

The *ba'al teshuvah* movement has changed the traditional patterns of passing observance down through the generations. Before, when the parents were more traditional, it was almost expected that the kids would assimilate. Yet, the children could always return to their parents' homes to eat. Now, however, the kids, the *ba'alei teshuvah*, cannot return to their parents' dining tables, won't "just once" eat their old favorite spareribs. Family pictures are evidence of a lifestyle rejected: birthday parties celebrated at restaurants the children will no longer frequent, people who are no longer what they once were.

The real people in this book—observant, non-observant, rabbis, laypeople—span the entire spectrum. There are those individuals whose emotional generosity is humbling and those whose pain is palpable. It is my only hope that we can all learn from each other.

Part I

The Families Speak

INTRODUCTION

*S*everal years ago, my daughter, then about five years old, was playing a board game with her observant cousin, who was the same age. Talia, my daughter, rolled the dice but, alas, did not roll the number that she needed for the game. Her cousin's immediate response was, "I guess *HaShem* didn't answer your prayers."

Talia had a truly dumbfounded look on her face. *HaShem* has no role in throwing the dice at our Conservative house. In fact, we generally don't speak of *HaShem*, or God, playing a part in the myriad details of ordinary life. Although my husband and I believe that we talk of ethics and values in all manner of daily events (e.g., "white lies" to friends, gossip, and so forth), *HaShem*, by name, usually shows up just in time to light candles for *Shabbat* dinner.

This regular talk of *HaShem* by *ba'alei teshuvah* makes many of their parents uncomfortable. Why are their rational, secularly educated professional children using this mumbo jumbo?

In addition to the discomfort that some parents feel with the talk of *HaShem* and the regular recitation of prayers, many parents express anxiety about the Orthodox garb. In our family, this issue came into play each time my sister-in-law became pregnant.

My observant brother and his wife have four children, the first three daughters. When my sister-in-law became pregnant with their fourth child, my mother said that she hoped that they would have another girl. It had nothing to do with passing down clothing or anxiety about a *bris*. Rather, little girls are invisibly Orthodox. They can go to the circus without being identified as Jews. Little Orthodox boys wear *kipot*.

For many people, religion is supposed to be private. Some parents worry that Jewish observance will interfere with the ability to compete in the workplace. After all, there are all those Jewish holidays that "regular" Jews don't take off. And can you leave early every Friday afternoon without engendering resentment? As one non-observant parent told his *ba'al teshuvah* son: "The real world doesn't operate that way and you have to live in the real world. Mixing religion with business is very dangerous."

For other parents, the worry of anti-Semitism lies just below the surface. Some of this fear may be characterized as self-hatred, but for vast majority of parents, the concerns are sincere and perhaps well founded.

And then, there are those parents and siblings who are truly perplexed by the Orthodox lifestyle—the triumphalism of some of the Orthodox rabbis, the seeming hypocrisy of the Orthodox lifestyle when some *mitzvot* are observed while others are not, and the general feeling of distance and loss that occurs when someone changes.

In this section, Naomi Rothberg discusses the reactions of friends and relatives to her son's Orthodoxy, Millicent Friedman describes how an Orthodox rabbi "secretly" arranged a bar mitzvah for her son three months prior to the scheduled Reform ceremony, Elizabeth Sandler talks of bug zappers on *Shabbat*, and Jim Estin tells of the pain he felt when his Orthodox sister would not recognize his daughter's bat mitzvah. An anonymous grandma tells how she decided to stop wearing jeans when visiting her daughter so that her grandchildren wouldn't get teased. Joan Levine laments the loss of art for her Orthodox grandchildren, while Rhonda Slater describes the mourning period after her father's unexpected death when she and her observant brother could not even share a meal. And, finally, Lynn Geller describes how the pace of Orthodox life makes it difficult for her to be close to her observant brother.

1

BRUSHING
IT OFF
Naomi Rothberg

*W*hen our son started to show an interest in religion, I assumed he was having a psychotic break. I was terrified, for him and for us.

Looking back, it is hard for me to separate this first interest in Judaism from his first interest in Israel, though I know Judaism came earlier. Maybe we didn't "come out" among our friends and family until the two were joined, and our son was actually talking about going to, that is, moving to, making a home in, Israel. (He was then 18, and a freshman at Columbia University.)

In any event, reaction from friends and family was to both Judaism and Israel together. It ranged from the sort of stunned silence that might be expected to greet the news that he was discovered to be a serial killer, to explosions of protest: "Not possible . . . how could he . . .

what are you doing about it . . ." One woman I knew well clutched my hands and cried, "Then he's *lost* to you!!"

Afterward came the more "considered" denunciations of religion—a crutch for the emotionally lame; a dangerous fanaticism; socially, morally retrograde—and of Israel as a racist, imperialist, fascist state. Of specific Jewish practices: "The *bris* is so utterly barbaric." "You mean the *bread* has to be kosher?" There were reasonably good friends we stopped seeing because they couldn't learn to keep their mouths shut. I wanted to kill all these people, even the ones I loved.

Then there were those met casually who, on learning our son lived in Israel, would beam: "Oh, you must be so proud!" And I wanted to kill them, too.

It is now thirteen years later. Shaiya (born Matthew Isaiah, now Yishayahu or Shaiya) continues to live in Israel, where he has a family of his own. My husband and I have long since ceased mourning or fearing that we would lose him. We are, in fact, very close (shuttling back and forth over all those miles by plane and phone and e-mail). And we consider him quite splendid, and we are kind of puffed up about being his parents. (Oh, if I could tell you all the marvelous things he does and is!!) But we will never be finished, it seems, with people otherwise close to us expressing shock and dismay that I *kasher* my kitchen before a visit from "the kids," that those kids really really truly *still* aren't going to drive to see them on a Saturday. That even the bread has to be kosher. That our older grandson, at age three, started wearing a *kipa* and *tzitzit*. And I will never, it seems, cease to be informed that religion is a crutch for the weak and that Israel is a monster state. You might think by now I could brush it off. But I can't.

2

HITTING
THE CEILING
Millicent Friedman

*M*y husband came from an Orthodox home on
the Lower East Side; I grew up in a non-observant home,
but I knew I was Jewish. My mother wouldn't permit me
to date anyone who wasn't Jewish, but I don't ever
remember having a Seder at home or celebrating any of
the holidays. We used to hang Christmas stockings by the
dumbwaiter door.

My mother was born in Poland, came here at age
fourteen, and was very intent on becoming as American-
ized as she could. But when her housekeeper suggested
that we put up a Christmas tree, that's where my mother
drew the line.

My Jewish involvement started when I was in college. During World War II, there were no boys around, no
dates, so I joined Junior Hadassah and a whole world

opened up for me. When my husband and I were married in 1948, we joined the "Mr. & Mrs." club at the Free Synagogue in Westchester, a Reform synagogue, in order to meet people. We formally joined the synagogue in 1950, after our daughter, Rose, was born. We were very active and by 1976, my husband was president of the congregation.

When our son David was in the fifth or sixth grade, he started going to Saturday morning services at an Orthodox synagogue with a friend, a boy named Alan Gordon. At that synagogue, the rabbi had a son, a boy about sixteen or seventeen years old. There was actually a group of young men who took these two younger boys under their wings. The younger boys were flattered that these older boys were paying attention to them.

Although my son absolutely loved it, we were not only worried, we were upset. I knew he was an extraordinary young man, a bright young boy. I would like to have channeled his interest toward a more liberal Judaism. Then an incident happened when David was preparing for his bar mitzvah at our synagogue.

David's birthday is February 4, and that was the middle of my husband's tax season; he was an attorney and an accountant. We decided to wait to have David's bar mitzvah until after tax season, in April. The Orthodox rabbi said no way, and he made David a bar mitzvah at his own synagogue and never informed us that he'd done it. We found out because members of the community were surprised that we weren't there. Well, let me tell you, I think I can still see the dent in the ceiling where my husband hit it. We were very upset. After all, his parents were alive. Not to ask our permission and not to invite us?

It got back to the rabbi that we were angry. He did apologize. I don't remember how the peace pact came about, but a few weeks after that, David was asked to participate in the *Shabbat* morning service at the Orthodox synagogue and the rabbi asked us to come, and we sponsored the *oneg shabbat*. The incident was papered over.

Everything came to a head, however, when David said he didn't want to attend the regular public high school and that he wanted to go to Yeshiva University High School for Boys in Washington Heights. I was a schoolteacher in the public system, a speech and language therapist. My husband and I were both public school advocates. David was adamant. We were adamant. There were many arguments and it wasn't a very pleasant time.

This went on for months. Then David came home one day and said, "The rabbi said that since you and Daddy don't want to send me to Yeshiva University High School, his congregation is going to run a raffle to pay my tuition." We were appalled! What would this look like? Lou and Millicent Friedman—*nebech*—they have to have a raffle for their son's tuition? By this time, we realized already that it was a losing battle and we acquiesced.

In high school, David was competing against boys who'd had lifelong education in yeshivas. He didn't have the background, so they put him in a "catch-up" class for a year. David was determined to catch up and he worked and studied until he was able to transfer to regular classes at the end of the first semester. He graduated eleventh out of 122 kids in the class and won the prize that was awarded to the young man who got the most out of the four years at Yeshiva University High School.

David had complained to his rabbi, Rabbi Solomon Freilach of Congregation Brothers of Israel in Mount Vernon, that we weren't kosher. The rabbi told him that it's true, you should be eating kosher, but the Bible says to honor thy father and mother and that comes before everything else. The rabbi didn't want to antagonize us and he wanted to hold onto David. I said to David, "You want me to respect you. You have to respect me. I'm a modern Reform Jew. I don't believe in *kashrut*. I will not blatantly antagonize you with bacon and ham but this is what I believe."

At first, I would buy kosher meat for just David, but then I bought kosher meat for everyone. But I didn't change my dishes. I didn't change my pots and pans.

After high school, David went to Israel for three years. When he came home, I went an extra step. I bought two sets of glass dishes, for meat and dairy, and silverware and pots and pans. I did cook his food separately for about a year before he married.

I absolutely adore my daughter-in-law. They have seven children and she is such a fantastic young woman. Unbelievable. I wouldn't have wanted anyone else for David. David is now a rabbi with his own congregation in Long Island.

My daughter Rose is married to Paul, a wonderful Jewish man. She's a "cardiac Jew," a Jew in her heart. She doesn't belong to a congregation. My son Seth lived in Israel for ten years and he is married to Robin, who comes from a very observant Conservative family—*shomer Shabbat* and kosher. They have four children. All of my eleven grandchildren go to religious day schools.

The relationship among my kids is not as warm as I want it to be. I try to get them together at Thanksgiving and during Chanukah. Perhaps, with my passing, it will bring them together . . . maybe not.

When you take a look at the larger picture, what would have been gained by holding a grudge, creating animosity? You diminish yourself with anger and animosity. This way, I am comfortable with my children and in my community. When I see Rabbi Freilach, we are good friends. He adores my son. I don't see what's gained by being unforgiving. It wouldn't change anything. It's so much more pleasant this way. Animosity tends to hurt not only the person to whom it's directed, but it eats away at the person who's angry. We're on this earth for such a short time; it's such a shame to waste it on bitterness. I'm 72 years old. That doesn't mean I haven't been angry in my lifetime or had ill thoughts toward people, but I've found that, as I look back, I haven't gained anything by it. It doesn't add anything to my life.

My son is following a path that will give him a sense of fulfillment. Isn't that what we want for our children?

3

CRAZY *FRUM*
Elizabeth Sandler

*I*f I were asked to define myself, the first word I would use would be *Jewish*. We are a Jewish family. Our daughter-in-law and two sons-in-law are Jewish. Our grandchildren all go to Jewish day schools or are homeschooled in a program that includes Hebrew and Jewish studies. Yet, half of us live an Orthodox religious life, half do not. In our own way, we reflect the plurality that defines the Jewish people at large. And similar to the Jewish communities at large, we recognize we are one family; we enjoy each other's company, but we have difficulty accommodating and accepting the differences among us.

Like parents and grandparents everywhere, we looked forward to our children growing, having children of their own, and gathering together for holidays to celebrate and share together. Our children live great distances from us, so we knew the gatherings would be infrequent. In our fantasies, they would center around the table where, in time-honored tradition, we would share food and stories and each other's company. It didn't turn out quite that way.

Our first inkling of the difficulties we would face came nineteen years ago. Our daughter and her fiancé were visiting us one Saturday. Shortly before guests of theirs were due to arrive at our house, I remembered the weeds along the driveway that needed to be cut to prevent cars from being scratched. I asked my daughter to trim the weeds. The answer was an inaudible mumble. With faces averted, the two young people headed out the door . . . empty-handed. I ran down and cut the weeds myself, barely controlling my anger. When the guests left that evening, I bellowed about what I considered a lack of consideration for others. I was informed that one didn't cut weeds on *Shabbat*. It was my first introduction to the fact that the young couple, our daughter and her fiancé, planned to live an Orthodox Jewish life and what that might mean. Since then, our life has been a roller coaster of ups and downs in the attempt to come to terms with what it means to have children who are Orthodox when we are not.

The advent of Orthodoxy for our oldest child was a gradual one and, it seems to me, is still a work in progress. Once married, our daughter and her husband settled into their home. Our son-in-law explored more deeply into the Jewish religion. Our daughter kept *Shabbat* and a kosher vegetarian kitchen, vegetarian to obviate the need for separate dishes. With the birth of our first grandchild a few years later, the family began to introduce more halachic rules. With each subsequent visit—they to us, we to them—new rituals were added. Then, as our first grandson approached his second birthday, our son-in-law mentioned that the child was getting old enough to understand, and because our house wasn't kosher . . . I burst into tears. It was the first time I realized that the grandchildren might be kept from visiting us if we didn't comply with the new rules.

The rules themselves seem to have an arbitrary element. *Hechshers* that were good last year are no longer kosher. New ones are introduced. When I go to services with my children, the *meheetzah* in one Orthodox synagogue is a low wall separating a slightly raised area from the main floor. Men and women see each other and sometimes converse before and after services. Not all married women cover their heads. When the Torah is taken around, it is brought near the wall so women may kiss the *siddurs* with which they touch the Torah. Yet, in a synagogue just a mile away, the women's section is a spacious second story balcony. For these women, there is no access to the Torah, although the women can observe the service below. In a third synagogue, in another city where my grandson was bar mitzvah, the women are confined to a small, second floor balcony that is separated by a very thick curtain from the floor below. It was impossible to see or to hear my grandson, or anyone else. I never met the rabbi. I have no idea what he looks like. All three synagogues are Orthodox.

No matter how much I read, I cannot figure things out. I had come to understand *Shabbat* in a way that I refer to as "a time out of time," a concept that I felt had a very beautiful meaning. Shortly after, I flew to one of our children's houses for a weekend. On *Shabbat*, I was surprised to hear an electric bug killer in active operation on the patio, emitting frequent sounds of bugs being incinerated by the electric coil. I asked, in honest curiosity, expecting a halachic explanation, how that fit in with a halachic view of *Shabbat*. I was told that it didn't, but they were doing it because they didn't want the bugs to get into the house.

For us, it is of primary consideration that our home be "home" to all of our children. To do this, we have finally purchased complete double sets of dishes, flatware, pots, and pans. When our Orthodox children visit, we clear our utensils out of the kitchen, cover the surfaces, and put in the kosher separated objects. We *kasher* the oven, stove, and microwave, and when the children arrive, we step out of the kitchen for the duration of their visit. We plan our weekends so that the *shomer Shabbat* families will have company, and we try to have times when the kosher and non-kosher contingents of the family are all together. The grandchildren are all bonded to each other, and the non-observant grandchildren, though it is not always easy, try to comply with the needs of the observant grandchildren.

It is difficult for our younger daughter and her family, the non-observant members of the family. When her observant siblings are visiting us, she cannot be as free in our kitchen as she normally is. On *Shabbat*, it means not being able to play with cousins in certain ways. For my non-observant daughter, it also means that her own friends feel more at ease in her home than do her siblings.

Though I will never live an Orthodox life, through extensive reading I have come to appreciate the philosophical underpinnings of many of the rituals. I think I understand what my children are trying to feel, trying to do, in a religious sense. Though I resent a *meheetzah,* I find going to services with my children can be nice as long as it is not a synagogue in which I feel totally excluded. My grandchildren, by the way, know my feelings about *meheetzahs.* They are tolerant of my thinking.

There's a tremendous need for more open communication between parents and children about these issues. And there's a need for better communication between observant and non-observant children. If there are going to be such divergent ways of operating, and these ways impinge upon the others who will be there, I feel there is a responsibility for the observant to engage in conversation to explain what will happen, and why it will happen. To assume one will "go along" with everything is incorrect and engenders a sense of being controlled. There need to be areas where one can choose to engage or not. For example, may I choose not to ritually wash my hands before eating *Shabbat* dinner so that I needn't face the dirty dishes in the sink? If it is important to the observant, perhaps there is a compromise. Perhaps a laver can be brought to the table area and the ritual performed there. If certain rituals are not mandatory in a house, can the guests be informed of that?

When my husband and I find ourselves totally confused about what to do, a story from our past comes to the fore and brings the perspective of humor back into our lives. Our best friends were getting married, and their respective elderly Jewish grandmothers met for the first time. In our friends' living room, both "bubbies" were seated on a couch. Each one stared straight ahead. Finally, one turned to the other and in a heavy accent asked, "You keep kosher?" "Sure," came the equally accented reply. "And you?" "*Vu den*? Of course!" There was a long pause as the grandmothers once more turned their heads to the front and silently stared straight ahead. A head turned and the second grandmother asked, "You drive on *Shabbos*?" "No. You?" "No." Both women returned to the contemplation of the wall in front of them. The silence was finally broken by a third question. "You answer the phone on *Shabbos*?" "Sure. And you?" "No, I don't answer the phone on *Shabbos*." "You don't?" asked the grandmother incredulously. "That's *crazy frum!*"

We remember the story, we laugh, and then we go on trying to integrate all the many facets of our family.

4

NO BRIDGES ACROSS
Jim Estin

*W*hen my sister Linda moved to Israel and started to become observant, I minimized the impact of the difference between her traditional Jewish life and my liberal Jewish one. I saw it as a different version of something similar, as opposed to something really very different. As time has gone on, however, I see it as more and more different.

Linda has always had strong opinions, not exactly self-righteous or extremist, but strong opinions. Over the last six or seven years, she's begun to use language that's very strong. I don't think she recognizes that she is the one who has changed. It's very apparent, though, in conversations we've had, for example, about God, the idea of God in her daily life. *HaShem* was not a part of her daily life when we were growing up.

My wife, Ann, is not Jewish, but her degree of involvement in the Jewish community is quite high. Early in our relationship, it was clear to me that my family had to be Jewish, and we've been very lucky in being able to associate with active and vibrant Jewish communities that were encouraging of that.

Two years ago, my daughter, Mira, celebrated her bat mitzvah at our Reform synagogue. It was very clear that Linda would not come to the United States for the bat mitzvah. She couldn't afford it but, more importantly, she wouldn't attend a service in a Reform synagogue. A few months before the bat mitzvah, however, I told Linda that I would like her to acknowledge Mira's bat mitzvah in some way. She sent Mira a birthday card.

Several months later, I attended the bar mitzvah of an Orthodox cousin in Milwaukee. When I returned home, I sent Linda an e-mail about the event. She wrote back, asking questions, wanting to know what I'd liked, all the details. I couldn't answer her because, at that point, I was hurt. It was such a pointed contrast to her total lack of curiosity about Mira's bat mitzvah.

Linda does not see my children as Jewish in any sense of the word. There's no acknowledgment of my daughter's Jewish knowledge, much less her sense of identity.

I had been Linda's strongest supporter when she married and became observant. I'm the only one of four siblings who visited her in Israel. Ann and I were the ones who shopped for the paper plates and kosher food for Linda's visits here. When our mother died, I was particularly sensitive to Linda's desires about the funeral service. And yet, now, I see only increasing distance between my family and Linda's family. I thought it could work out. I assumed I'd be the bridge with Linda. But, ultimately, there probably are no bridges.

5

"YOUR *SAFTA* WEARS PANTS?"

Anonymous

Question: How would you characterize your home when your three daughters were growing up?

Answer: Normal. We considered ourselves ethical Jews. We ate bacon and didn't light candles but we considered ourselves Jewish.

Question: Did your oldest daughter, the one who has become Orthodox, have any formal Jewish education?

Answer: No, she didn't. She didn't want to go to Sunday school but my younger two were confirmed. We belonged to a Reform synagogue. We hung up stockings on the fireplace and gave everybody Christmas and Chanukah presents.

Question: When did your oldest daughter first show any interest in Judaism?

Answer: She was a student at Dartmouth. She was dating some guy, probably her first Jewish boyfriend, and they were talking about how some Orthodox Jews consider the earth flat. Later, she got a job teaching math at a Catholic girl's school. The sisters wanted her to go to Catholic services. She didn't need to pray; she just had to go. As a rebellion against that, she joined a little synagogue. She used to tell me about her interest in Jewish cooking.

Then, in 1983, my husband died. At that time, I was more active in Reconstructionism. We had a very nice funeral but my daughter was upset. The next thing I knew, she wanted to go to Israel and study at a yeshiva, a woman's yeshiva. So she studied and learned. And I was a little annoyed because I thought, "Hurry up and come home. It's enough nonsense already." Then she called and told me she'd met a nice man and she was thinking about getting married.

Question: Was her fiancé also an American?

Answer: He's British, a convert to Judaism, with a Catholic mother and a Jewish father. He had been raised a Catholic, but when his father died, his mother asked him to arrange for a Jewish funeral. He went through an Orthodox conversion and was circumcised at the age of twenty-three. When they got married, she was twenty-five and he was twenty-seven. They weren't kids. I used to tease them that I've never seen two people walk closer without touching.

Question: Did you go to the wedding?

Answer: Oh, yes. I bought a dress with long sleeves and I found a hat. We had a nice contingent from the United States. I thought it was pretty crazy. I kept thinking, "She'll get over this." But she never did.

Question: What is their family like now?

Answer: My daughter is very happy and I adore my son-in-law. He and my daughter are both very funny people. After they got married, my son-in-law started doing some teaching and writing, and my daughter went to work for a publishing company. They're pretty much independent. They have six children. The oldest is fourteen.

Question: How often do you see them?

Answer: At least once a year. The last time they were here they had three kids. It's easier for me to go to Israel. I try to get there when my daughter is having a baby and on the "off years" I go and have fun.

Question: What has been the reaction of your other daughters?

Answer: Mixed. My Orthodox daughter disapproved when my youngest daughter married a non-Jew and she disapproved when they had a little boy and didn't circumcise him. My youngest daughter would have loved her big sister to have approved of her husband but it didn't work out that way. Right now my youngest daughter is divorced. Are they close? Not really. They e-mail once or twice a year. We're planning to have a mini-family reunion in Jerusalem and my other two daughters are planning to come.

Question: When you go to Israel, what accommodations do you make?

Answer: When my daughter is having a baby, I do the cooking. It's not that difficult. All you have to do is keep the meat and milk separate. They have two sets of pots, with red tape or blue tape. I make mistakes but they don't scream at me. For example, on *Shabbat*, you have tea brewing and you have to pour it in a certain order—the tea first, then the hot water, not the reverse. I have to tear toilet paper in advance.

The first few years when I'd go over there, I thought, "The heck with it. I'll just wear my jeans." The kids at the park would laugh at me. I didn't want them to tease my grandchildren so now I take dresses. I don't cover my head, though. The other kids know that my grandchildren have a *safta* who doesn't cover her head.

I adore my son-in-law but I don't touch him. When I see him, I give him great big hugs in mid-air. I can hug my daughter and my grandchildren and the air in front of my son-in-law. I ask my son-in-law, "How old do I have to get to give you a hug?" He always jokingly tells me, "You will never be old enough to give me a hug."

Question: Has your attitude about Orthodoxy changed at all?

Answer: We laugh about it. I tell them, when the kids aren't there, that they're crazy. But *Shabbat* is a lovely time.

From Friday afternoon until late Saturday, to have time to read and walk and not work, it's lovely. I wish I could keep it here. There's a lot of stuff that makes sense with Orthodox Judaism. When you see a beautiful sight, you say a little prayer. If you see a healthy newborn baby, you say a prayer. There's even a prayer you say when you go to the bathroom. If you've ever been constipated or had a bladder problem, it makes sense.

I do sometimes make mistakes. One time I was reading a book to my grandkids about dolphins. I explained that they were land animals before they adapted. After I left, I got this very unhappy phone call from my daughter that I was teaching the kids evolution. I said I was sorry, that I didn't realize the Orthodox didn't accept the concept of evolution. I certainly don't want to antagonize my daughter or son-in-law and drive any wedges between me and my six wonderful grandchildren. I still think Orthodox Judaism is crazy, but I love my daughter and I love my grandchildren. I don't have any choice. I want them to love me. It's not that big a deal. I can get along in their society very well and in so doing, really enjoy them. You can't dictate what your kids do. Loving your kids and being close to them is so much more important.

6

SHTETL **BLINDERS**
Joan S. Levine

Dear Son:

When people come into your home in Jerusalem and see my Zayda's picture, taken when he was a young man, they think it is a picture of you. You love the connection, which I love, too. Yet, your observant style of life, though I tremendously admire its high morality and faithfulness, brings me pain.

I have a strong memory of sitting outside the Israel Museum several years ago, caring for my then three-year-old and almost one-year-old (of blessed memory) grandsons, so that their mother, the artist, could go in with the older girls to see the Rembrandt exhibit. It was a wonderful exhibit, showing Rembrandt's use of the stories in the Torah, set into his time frame.

I thought your wife would enjoy the artistry and technique in the painting. You had reservations about it, because you were afraid there was too much immodesty in the paintings of the women, and you didn't like Rembrandt's interpretations of the all of the Judaica.

The pain I felt, and feel, is from the fact that you had exposure to great art, music, and drama, which your wife also had. You are a superior musician, and she is an excellent artist. You both made your own choices as to how to live your lives, but you are also making *their* choices. Your children are not being given choices. They will never enjoy the art of the kinds I just saw at the major London galleries. They will never sit and watch a symphony orchestra, which might be composed of both men and women. They will see segregated performances, which may be well done, but you have closed their eyes and ears to the world of art, music, and drama, a world that could be depicting man's struggle to become a better human being, kinder and gentler to his fellows.

We live in a world of instant communication, which can bring museums into our houses with a CD Rom. We can watch Jewish conductors, playing music they have written, and Jewish performers bringing the spirit of our religion into the music they perform; but you have put nineteenth-century *shtetl* blinders onto your children.

They are well versed in Torah and ritual, and the joys and pains of observance, but my fear is that they will not be well versed in how to survive in the world as it will be for their adult years. My Zayda was a well-educated man, observant, knowledgeable in Torah and Jewish literature. One of your grandfathers was an educated dentist, one grandmother a college graduate who took fifteen years to get her degree.

Your father is an excellent physician, and I have a master's degree and have taught for thirty years. My mother, my cousins, and I have had to make a living in the real world, a living that helps to enable you to live as you do. Will my granddaughters be able to be self-sufficient if need presents itself? Will my grandsons be able to provide for a family and know about the world around them, so that they, and their sisters, are not locked out of the world?

Dear son, these thoughts are why I sometimes feel like an alien to you, and you to me. I love you very much. The world is wide and can be wonderful. The arts of the world are what help us to be above the animals, and they can enrich our lives and our senses for all kinds of learning. Forgive me if I am denying your feelings, but I had to try to express mine to you.

With love,
Mom

7

MOURNING
THE LOSS
Rhonda Slater

*M*y younger brother is Orthodox and has lived in the West Bank of Israel since his wedding in 1981. He has studied in both Los Angeles and Israel and, although he is not a pulpit rabbi, he has enough schooling to enjoy the title of rabbi. Though we were very close as children, we have grown quite distant. When my brother's life was going down such a different path than what I was used to, I felt pushed away.

One of the most vivid instances occurred when our father passed away suddenly, at the age of 58. Since our parents were divorced, the responsibility of making his funeral arrangements fell on us, his four children. I remember calling my brother in Israel to tell him of our father's death. His first words were not words of comfort but orders—how we had to bury him, what rituals needed to be followed, what kind of coffin we needed to purchase. Not only was I feeling the extreme loss of my father but, in a way, I was also feeling the loss of my brother.

My father died on a Sunday but we had the funeral on Tuesday, as we needed to wait until my brother flew in from Israel and my younger sister came in from New York. At the time, I had two small babies; one was two-years-old and the other was six-months-old. Between the loss of my father and the responsibility of taking care of my sons, I was overwhelmed.

As soon as my brother arrived, he started barking orders again. On the morning of the funeral, my sister wanted to see my father for one last time. My brother was very upset with the fact that she wanted to open the casket. He finally agreed but with two conditions: only for a few minutes, and no one else would be allowed in. My husband did go in the room, however, because he wanted to put some pictures of our family, along with some personal items, in the casket.

After the service, we waited until the hundreds of people passed by. After they had left the funeral chapel, we walked over to where the casket was to be buried. As I walked to the chairs for the family, I was astonished by how many people were at the graveside.

I am *sure* that I had told my brother that I did not want to be there when they started throwing the dirt on the coffin. Yet, the next thing I knew, I was hearing the pounding of the dirt as it fell onto the box. I became hysterical. To this day, I can still hear that awful sound playing in my head. Now, many years later, I understand the *mitzvah* of throwing dirt onto the coffin, but no one explained it then.

When we went back to my father's apartment to receive our friends and family, we mourned our loss in different ways. My brother, along with all of his Orthodox friends and rabbis, went into my father's bedroom while the rest of us walked around the apartment. We felt so isolated from our brother. Even the food that we were eating was separated, kosher and not kosher.

This is not the only time that I have felt so distanced from my brother, but it is the most vivid memory I have. Perhaps, if he lived closer, it would afford us more opportunities to discuss our different values, morals, and life choices. My brother has been back to the States several times over the past eighteen years, but there never seems to be much time to talk. I do feel sorry that our lives have taken us so far apart, that our children don't even know their cousins, aunts, and uncles. It is very difficult to maintain a close relationship with people who are so different, even though of the same religion. I feel that my brother's deep convictions have taken him away from us, not only in physical distance but in mental acceptance as well.

8

TUMULT
OR TRADITION?
An interview with Lynn Geller

Question: You have four older brothers, three of whom are observant. You are not observant. Are you close to your brothers?

Answer: One of my observant brothers, David, lives nearby and has a five-year-old daughter. My husband and I have two daughters, aged two and five. But it's difficult to be close, in part because the pace of their lives is so different from ours.

For most observant families, the focus is on *Shabbat*. The women in their community are reinforced by their husbands for accomplishing everything and being exhausted by the end of the week. The hour before *Shabbat* is crazy. You probably need *Shabbat* if you're that busy during the hours before.

Then, it's *Shabbat*. They think nothing of sitting at the *Shabbat* dinner table for hours and hours. The fact that they have children to care for doesn't seem important. My niece, for example, falls asleep on the couch.

My husband and I are raising our children fairly strictly, with routines that include going to bed early. We, too, have *Shabbat* dinner, but we conclude relatively quickly so that the children can go to bed on time, in their beds, not on the couch.

We don't want our children to stay up to all hours on Friday night, especially in the summer when *Shabbat* starts late. Since our families' schedules are very different, it makes it difficult to share *Shabbat* together in the summer.

My husband and I find it easiest to get together with friends and family on a Sunday, late afternoon or early evening. My brother's family, however, has a lot to accomplish on Sundays since it is the only day for them to run errands. So while Judaism is meant to bring family together, in our case, it seems to keep us apart.

In many Orthodox families, it's much more of a *balegan*; it's a zoo. They don't have the routines and discipline we've chosen to have.

Question: How do you account for the lack of discipline you suggest?

Answer: They have so many things they have to do that the rest of us don't do. My brother gets up at 5 A.M. to study; I get up at 5 A.M. to exercise before work.

Maybe they have so many rules imposed on them that they can't handle any more rules. And our rules aren't as important as their rules.

In years past, I've made all the effort. They make the rules and I make all the effort to accommodate their rules.

I do paper plates; I double wrap baked potatoes. But now . . . I've had enough.

To give another example, Orthodox children are taught what they can and cannot eat, how to eat, how to pray, and so on. This is very good, but the children are not taught that there are Jews in the world who choose not to follow all the rules and that these Jews are still Jews. After my five-year-old daughter's birthday party this year, my niece came home with us so that my brother and sister-in-law could see a movie. My niece brought her own dinner since she is not allowed to eat our food. As I was cleaning up, my niece said, "Next week I get to go to another girl's birthday party. I don't have to bring my own food because they are Jewish." My heart sank as far as it could and I quickly responded by saying, "We are Jewish too. We just don't follow all the rules you do."

The discipline taught to Orthodox children is good to a point. However, the *mitzvah* of tolerance isn't taught early enough. In order to raise Orthodox children to be so focused and narrow, it means making sure they don't know about choices in life. Is it possible that the Orthodox could teach their children to be more open to the range of Jewish practice?

Part II

The *Ba'alei Teshuvah* Speak

INTRODUCTION

*W*hen it came time to celebrate my parents' fiftieth wedding anniversary, my brother Michael held the trump card. The most observant member of the family always holds the *kashrut* trump card since he or she can say, "I won't—or can't—come."

So, what's a family to do? If, for example, we chose to give a dinner party for my parents, inviting two hundred of their closest friends, the party would need to be held at either a kosher restaurant/hotel or at someone's house with a kosher caterer. Is it right to ask my non-observant brother Larry to pay one-third of the higher cost of a kosher caterer? If significant amounts of money are at stake, is it fair for the religious demands of one participant to trump the decisions?

We decided to send my parents on a trip to Europe.

It's not always that simple. One mother I interviewed is dealing with the ultra-Orthodoxy of her teenaged son. The family keeps kosher and is *shomer Shabbat*. Yet, the son would like more. When asked what he would wish for if he were to get three wishes, the boy said: "First, I wish that we could have two dishwashers, one *milchig* (milk) and one *fleishig* (meat). Second, I'd like to use only *Cholav Yisrael* milk products (specially supervised dairy products). Third, on *Pesach*—*gebrocht*. (*Gebrocht* is a practice, during Passover, where matzoh is never mixed with any liquid. This means no matzoh balls, no matzoh brei, and so on. The only exceptions are for the Hillel sandwich during the Seder and the last day of the eight-day holiday.)

On the particular day that I visited this family, it was a school holiday. It was also, coincidentally, a minor fast day in the Jewish calendar. Knowing it was a school holiday, the mom had made a dentist appointment for her son. He wouldn't go. Because it was a fast day, he was uncomfortable swallowing and spitting the water necessary to clean and examine his teeth. I watched as the mother telephoned the dentist to apologetically cancel the appointment. She turned to me and, in her normal, calm tone, said, "Don't think I'm not aggravated."

Siblings are enormously affected when a young adult, still living at home, becomes observant. As the parents attempt to accommodate the newly observant child, life changes for the siblings. One fourteen-year-old, whose older brother has become very observant, says, "At first I was mad. Because of him, we couldn't order pizza anymore. We couldn't get any good food. When I go to bar mitzvah parties and I'm dancing with someone, he comes up with a balloon and sticks it between us. Sometimes it makes me want to rebel against Judaism." The youngest child in the family, an eleven-year-old girl, laments, "I'd like to stay at the same stage I am and it's, like, all of a sudden, the past two years, everything has been changing."

Observance, thus, becomes, or is perceived as, power and control. Some *ba'alei teshuvah* are uncomfortable with the demands they must make on their families. Others, however, are insensitive to the impact their Judaism has on the people around them.

In this section, the *ba'alei teshuvah* speak. Marsha Arons tells of the time, during Passover, when her mother-in-law wanted to use a grapefruit knife that was in a sealed kitchen drawer. Alex Polonsky describes the first Thanksgiving dinner after he decided to keep kosher. Michael Stein writes about the legitimacy of Jewish identity. Singer/songwriter Peter Himmelman and his mother dialogue about his observance and their relationship.

Two contributors, Brent Baer and Alan Perlman, share letters that they wrote to their parents. Gary Kornfeld describes how, for his father, Judaism is "the other woman." Rita Schwartz Singer answers the Frequently Asked Questions (FAQs) that *ba'alei teshuvah* are asked. And, finally, Yosef Branse describes a final *mitzvah* performed by his atheist father.

9

OF GRAPEFRUIT KNIVES, GRANDMAS, AND GRACIOUSNESS

Marsha Arons

*W*hen my husband and I met and married almost twenty-three years ago, we made some important decisions together about the type of lifestyle we intended to have. We knew we wanted to create a warm, loving family where both of us as parents could be involved to a great extent in our children's daily lives. We knew we wanted to live in a safe, comfortable house, large enough to accommodate our family but not so large that we couldn't clean all the bathrooms ourselves. And we knew we wanted to live in a suburban neighborhood close enough to a large city to take advantage of cultural and educational opportunities. All those goals were supported by our families because they were pretty much the same experiences that our parents had given us.

But what surprised everyone at first, then later

provoked some negative and, at times, hostile reactions was our choice to become more religiously knowledgeable and observant. Our reasons for becoming observant were and are intensely personal. One of my major motivations was the fact that just as I married, I became an orphan; my father had died when I was eighteen, and my mother died ten days after my wedding, when I was twenty-two. I felt cut adrift even though I was embarking on a lifelong road with the man I loved. But he represented my future. I no longer had much tie to my past and that connection was important to me.

So we set up a kosher home, learning the rules along the way. And as each of our four daughters was born and went to day school, we learned along with them. Each simple act we performed—entering a room, eating, going to sleep at night—was imbued with religious ritual. We kissed the *mezuzahs*, made the proper blessing over what we ate, and said *Shema* (the prayer that proclaims God's uniqueness). And each time, we felt connected, not just to our immediate past but to thousands of years of Jewish life and the Jews who were our ancestors. We felt continuity.

But our family—our extended family—felt something else. They felt threatened. In some ways, I think they felt that as our little nuclear family moved closer to Judaism, we were moving farther away from them. And it seemed that they also thought that if we felt so strongly that what we were doing was right, then it must follow that we thought that what they did or didn't do was wrong.

But the one thing our family has always had going for it is our love for, and genuine enjoyment of, one another. My husband's parents were the quintessential grandma and grandpa—loving, doting, unapologetically spoiling our children. And the children thrived on this unconditional love made more precious by the fact that their grandparents lived in New Jersey and we lived in Chicago. All of my husband's siblings and mine live in different cities from us. Our phone bills and airfares are testament to the fact that the distance is only geographic.

During our sixth year of marriage, my husband's father died. Our two oldest children were four and one. It seemed to me that my mother-in-law, though devastated by her own grief, felt an increased responsibility toward our children because she had become their only grandparent. She made sure that she continued to be a beloved and vital part of their lives. We visited as often as possible and the children each took a turn clamoring for "my turn to talk to Gram" during our frequent phone conversations. Our children delighted in relating each milestone and accomplishment to the one person they knew would always be as proud of their effort and happy for their achievement as we, their parents, were. What exists between my children and their grandmother is precious.

That bond, and our commitment to nurturing it, made it easier to deal with the inevitable questions my daughters asked as they became old enough: "We do this; why doesn't Gram?" And even "Is Gram Jewish?" (This from a preschooler.) What I never heard was, "Why do we do this if Gram doesn't?" That was very significant to us because it meant to us that our children weren't questioning who *they* were. They were comfortable with their Jewish identities. At times, they even felt sorry for Gram, who didn't get to share in the beauty and joy of their observance of *Shabbat* or one of the holidays. I answered my children's questions by talking about choices. I talked also about respecting and loving parents and grandparents just because of who they are. In my mother-in-law's case, my children had no trouble understanding this concept.

But as our children got older, they and we learned more and sought higher levels of observance. And inevitably, each new stage would provoke some remark from a secular relative. I heard comments like, "I'm going to Belgium and they have that fabulous chocolate I'd like to bring back for you if it's kosher *enough*." Or, "I can get front row tickets to that new play and Kayla (daughter number three) would love it. Can you make an exception about Friday night *just this once*?" Or even, "We called and called you all day Saturday but you just wouldn't answer the phone. And we had something *so* important to tell you!" It seemed to me then that these relatives viewed our observance as an inconvenience for them and just a passing fad for us.

But time gives us new perspectives. Slowly, I began to see that our relatives' fears arose because they loved us and did not want to lose us. Once I understood that, it became easier not to view each small barb as devastating. And I remembered something my mother had once said to me in another context: None of us can change anyone else; we can only change our own reactions to what others do.

One Passover, I learned the truth of this. My mother-in-law had come to spend the week with us. By this time, we had been married about fifteen years and had three children. We were scrupulous about keeping kosher and *Shabbat*, and our level of enjoyment of the holidays had escalated along with our level of observance of it. Passover is my children's favorite holiday and despite all the preparation and work leading up to it, I love it too. I do have my own feelings that it should be observed once every four years for a month. I mean, if I'm going to all the trouble to clean that well and turn over my whole kitchen, the effort should be for a holiday that lasts longer than a week. I also admit that I find the cleaning and organizing somewhat cathartic, though I know that isn't the sort of spirituality associated with the holiday that the rabbis intended. But, that's only because they probably never had the satisfaction of finding four missing gloves at the back of the front hall closet—gloves that, despite the fact that many Passovers came and went, hadn't been seen since 1982.

That Passover, my children were thrilled that Gram had come so they could show off for her at the Seder and tease her about her red face after her four cups of wine. (They made sure she got the biggest Kiddush cup and filled it to the rim each time. Sweet red wine is her favorite.) And during the week, they couldn't seem to get enough of her matzoh balls. (It's a mix, but my kids think it tastes better when the balls are rolled with Gram's hands than when they are rolled with mine. They're right.)

Because my mother-in-law loves grapefruit, I made sure to have plenty on hand during her visit. One evening, she was helping herself to one but couldn't find a grapefruit knife among my Passover cutlery. After fifteen years of marriage, I had a pretty extensive array of Passover dishes, cutlery, pots, pans, and serving utensils. But, unfortunately, I did not have a Passover grapefruit knife. I had other knives, but none of them had the little serrated edge that my mother-in-law needed to section the grapefruit the way she liked it. As we stood looking at each other in the kitchen, I wondered how to resolve the situation.

My mother-in-law held up her hand and said, "I know!" She put her finger to her lips, then conspiratorially motioned me to follow her. She walked over to my everyday utensil drawer that was taped over, and she carefully pulled it open. She extracted the knife, made a sign of a cross over it, cut her grapefruit, washed the knife, put it back in the drawer, and reaffixed the tape.

I stood dumbfounded for a moment. But the look on her face was pure mischievous delight. I did what any religious-observant-respectful-loving daughter-in-law-and-mother-of-four-very-impressionable-children-whom-I-am-obligated-to-teach would do.

I laughed.

Lightning didn't strike us.

My mother-in-law's gesture was an antic. It wasn't meant to undermine me or my principles. And my children got the message: They didn't feel that it was okay to break the laws of Passover. And they weren't given the impression that their grandmother is a heretic. They just saw that we are a loving family and we can accommodate each other. They also saw that we don't have to take either ourselves or each other too seriously. What we *are* obligated to take seriously is the important stuff, such as the commandments to "Honor your father and mother" and the one that says "Do not do unto others that which is hateful to you."

So where are we now, approximately ten years after what we have come to refer to as "The Grapefruit Knife Caper"? We have become more observant. We moved to a *shomer Shabbat* community and my children attend Orthodox day schools. My husband covers his head at all times and I gave up wearing pants. We eat only kosher food and try hard to do what we know is required of us.

And we love and respect our family. Because that definitely is what is required of us.

Not very long ago, we took a vacation to visit my mother-in-law in Arizona. She had purchased a new set of pots for us. And she proudly showed me the *hechshers* on the canned goods that she had found in her local grocery store. She had taken the time to look for them instead of just buying the brands that were familiar to her. We ate a lot of tuna, boiled eggs, baked potatoes, fresh fruits, and vegetables while we were there.

And yes, indeed, we ate on paper plates.

The last night of our vacation in Arizona, my mother-in-law and I walked outside to the citrus tree in her backyard. I stood for just a moment in the fading light and inhaled the fragrance of citrus and wisteria, summer warmth and something else. We picked two grapefruits and took them inside.

Then, she using her knife and I using the new one that she had bought for me, we both proceeded to enjoy our fruit.

10

MODIM
Alex S. Polonsky

*T*hanksgiving. That crisp day in November when food and family converge. In my family, it is a holiday oblivious to religion. That fact never affected me until this past year, when for the first time since I started to keep kosher, my equally *ba'al teshuvah* fiancé and I showed up at my cousin's house for the traditional Thanksgiving meal. Every year my extended family attempts to coordinate their schedules to meet in New Jersey or New York, depending on which cousin is hosting. I am sure our gathering is similar to yours—non-stop hors d'oeuvres, turkey, stuffing, and endless pies and cakes that are never finished. Food is the center of the meal, but family remains the focus.

When you and your fiancé are the only ones keeping kosher, eating becomes more complicated. And I imagine that in a non-tolerant family, you could leave feeling that you have nothing to be thankful for. But in my family, there is tolerance, there is compromise, there is peace, and I find there is much *modim*—much thanksgiving.

"So, we want to make food for you here," my cousin Amy first broached the subject. I had two immediate thoughts. The first was guilt. I am the one who is taking on the yoke of Orthodox Judaism. Why should my cousin be going through the trouble of trying to accommodate me? My second thought was of my fiancé. It would be her first introduction to the family, and my first time keeping kosher in front of everyone.

I immediately wanted to say, "No!" It would be so much easier to just say no. All my protective emotions were welling up to give me the power to say, "No." I had silly thoughts. I felt that if I compromised my *kashrut* at Thanksgiving, in front of the whole family, that I would be on a slippery slope to eating bacon. "Where would it end?" I thought. Family would always say, "Well, he ate what Amy cooked at Thanksgiving, why won't he eat what I cooked?" Also, my fiancé would be there to both be scrutinized by my family and to scrutinize me in front of my family. "Not a good time to give up the cooking 'driver's seat' to my cousin," I thought. I can't remember what I told Amy, but we didn't make any concrete decision that night.

But what I forgot during that initial phone call was that my family is a master of compromise. I am not sure my family thinks of itself as a master of compromise, but from the stories my newly observant friends have told me, the Polonsky family gets an A+ in that category. The crux of the tolerance and compromise is that kosher isn't threatening when it is just another diet. My sister is a vegetarian, my father eats only low-cholesterol foods, my aunt is on a medically imposed "gluten-free" diet, and my fiancé and I keep kosher.

And no one passes judgment. No one views the dietary restriction as being unreasonable. For example, no one would say to my sister that it is more important for me to keep kosher than for her to avoid red meat. Each of us is dedicated to our diets for different but personally justified reasons, and no one attacks those reasons.

So what ended up happening? You can look at the menu (see page 59) that Amy printed to see how it all turned out: "K" stands for kosher and "G" stands for gluten-free. (My sister and dad knew which dishes were vegetarian or contained cholesterol, so there was no need to identify those dishes for them.) Amy and I went through each dish being prepared to see if we could make it kosher. If we couldn't, we moved on, accepting the fact that other non-kosher dishes were going to be served at the same table. Everyone also accepted that the adults would eat off nice china, but the kids, and my fiancé, and I would use disposable place settings. We appreciated the accommodation and thought nothing of the fact that we were using "kiddie" place settings. In fact, it felt like home since I eat off paper plates frequently at home. And no one was upset that we couldn't eat off their nice china. It seemed to be nothing special, yet at the same time, it was very special.

The beginning uncooked courses were easy. My aunt and uncle made kosher hummus from chick peas and techina. The same happened with the guacamole and the fruit cocktail with Ben & Jerry's sorbet. All the ingredients for the salad dressing were also kosher. The entrees were more difficult, and we made some major compromises. The baked potatoes and the string beans were cooked in Amy's kitchen, but in double-sealed aluminum foil and disposable, single-use tins. There was no compromise for the turkey, so my fiancé and I brought our own turkey, along with cranberry sauce and gravy, from a kosher deli.

So what did we learn? We could keep kosher while spending time with family if we were willing to eat from disposable place settings and have non-kosher food served at the same time. It seems so simple and in a way it was. But this situation has caused so much anxiety and emotional distancing among families. *Modim*. Be gratefully thankful.

Polonsky Thanksgiving Menu

Appetizers
Hummus with pita (K,G)
Guacamole with corn chips (K,G)
Baby carrots (K,G)
Bruscetta

First course
Mandarin orange fruit cocktail with sorbet
or
Fruit cocktail with Ben & Jerry's sorbet (K)

Salad
Spring greens and sundried tomatoes
with warm goat cheese balsamic vinaigrette
Spring greens and sundried tomatoes
dressed with raspberry vinaigrette (K,G)

Entrée
Grilled Turkey (G)
Herb Stuffing
Gravy (G)
Ivan's cranberry sauce (G)
Canned cranberry Sauce (G)
Steamed string beans (K,G)
Garlic roasted mashed potatoes (G)
Special mashed potatoes
Idaho baked potatoes (K)
Sweet potatoes (G)
Sweet potatoes topped with marshmallows
Creamed onions (G)
Hot spiced fruit compote (G)
Andrea's applesauces
Andrea's special applesauce (G)
Jay's homemade bread

Dessert
Barbara's kid treat
Andrea's pecan pie
Linda's pumpkin pie
Amy's key lime pie

11

TRADITION IS PERSONAL
Michael Stein

*W*e have a religious tradition that is shared by the entire Jewish people, but our experience of that tradition is intensely personal. Trying to make the tradition your own when you have no personal experience in it can elicit insecurity. In particular, if no childhood memories and experiences exist, a permanent emotional void exists.

It seems to me that one of the hardest emotional issues facing newly observant men and women is concern over the legitimacy of their own Jewish identity. Judaism has been passed down from generation to generation, and giving our children the sense that they are engaged in a spiritual quest alongside their parents, grandparents and great-grandparents is central to Judaism. The Passover Seder is a prime example, when continuity throughout the generations and the teaching of our children is explicitly emphasized. But all major holidays, and all life cycle events, bring with them traditions that are old and sacred.

For the newly observant, the times when family is most heavily emphasized by tradition are the same times when alienation from family is most acute. Just when we are celebrating the continuity of Jewish tradition, the newly observant have to set up fences between themselves and their families. To make matters worse, the Orthodox world, and especially the ultra-Orthodox world, is quite obsessed with legitimacy and authenticity. The *ba'al teshuvah's* secular family is a very public reminder at every important life cycle event that he or she has not had the benefit of a *frum*-from-birth upbringing, which can call into question the very legitimacy of his or her religious identity.

This is particularly sad, because in my opinion the Orthodox world, and especially the ultra-Orthodox world, suffers greatly due to an excessive and inappropriate emphasis on legitimacy. The religious world has its own insecurities to deal with, its own failure to cope better with modernity, and its own challenge to win over the hearts and minds of most Jews. In response, it has turned inward, become more insular and invented new strictures that would have surprised our ancestors from Europe. The newly observant sometimes unwittingly absorb that communal insecurity, combine it with their personal insecurities, and take it all out in their relationships with their more secular families.

The worst experience I recall with my non-observant family was when my mother actually made an attempt to serve us a kosher meal. I walked in quite late, and found my wife, Rachel, in tears, storming out of the house with our little baby in her arms. To this day I don't believe my mother has any idea as to why Rachel was upset.

My mother's efforts to serve an occasional kosher meal generally made things worse, not better. Every time she would try to accommodate our needs, she would ask questions as if she had never heard of *kashrut* before. It was so clearly an effort for her that it struck us as simply denial—denial due to an unending emotional hostility toward and resentment of my religious observances. My wife and I often felt that if she couldn't host us graciously, it would be better to not host us at all. But that seemed to be awfully petty on our part—shouldn't we be happy that my mother was making some effort rather than none? Guilt.

In the years before this incident, I had been much more extreme in my beliefs, and had said terribly hurtful things that I deeply regretted, particularly regarding my older brother's intermarriage. This created some basis for my mother's hostility toward my religious identity. But the entire family knew that her opposition to my religious life was rooted in its very existence—and in the fact that it threatened to take me to Israel and away from her. In fact, she once told me explicitly that if I moved to Israel, it would seem as if I were dead.

Anyway, I had tried to mend things with my brother and his wife, and at some juncture, my mother invited all of us to her home for a kosher meal. She bought the food in stores we specified, served everything on paper plates, and made the microwave kosher. It was a meat meal. Come dessert, I still hadn't arrived.

Apparently, my brother wanted ice cream for dessert. My mother knew she couldn't serve ice cream at the dining room table where everybody had eaten so, after a protracted give-and-take between my brother and mother (which Rachel, much to her discomfort, overheard), my mother served my brother ice cream in the kitchen. Very shortly, Rachel walked into the kitchen. The scene made her feel like a foreigner coming from the outside and forcing a bunch of people who didn't care at all about keeping kosher to jump through hoops they all resented.

To make matters worse, Rachel had never been the sort to preach or lecture others, and suddenly she was the Evil Enforcer. She didn't want to represent that kind of religion. She didn't want to force anyone to do anything. But she also didn't understand why ice cream was so important that my family would put her in that situation altogether.

I believe Rachel felt that my mother's hostility toward religion must be aimed at her as well. After all, my marriage to Rachel seemed to have solidified my permanent entry into an Orthodox world. I'm sure my absence at dinner only increased Rachel's sense of isolation. A complex and volatile mix of emotions welled up inside of her. That was when I walked in.

Sitting with Rachel in the car, parked in my parents' backyard, she explained to me how lonely and alienated she felt from my family, and how she didn't want to be the one forcing anything on them. My family probably thought, and may still think, that Rachel was outraged in principle at my brother eating milk after meat. I tried to explain to my father that Rachel's sense of belonging in our family was at stake, not some petty outrage at a violation of *kashrut* laws. To the contrary, she resented being put in the position of being the enforcer! I think my father did understand, but I don't think my mother ever figured it out. That was the last kosher meal she attempted to serve in her home for many years.

12

MOTHER AND SON

*From interviews with Beverly Fink
and her son Peter Himmelman*

Beverly: Peter was kicked out of Hebrew school because he talked too much. "How come your kids ask me those kinds of questions?" one teacher asked me.

Peter: I guess the most boring place in the world for me was always synagogue, and I still have trouble with it. But when I was in sixth grade in Hebrew school, these Lubavitchers came with a *Succah*-mobile. The passion that they had for what they were doing led me to believe—and I'm not kidding—that they were actors. They were dressed in old-world garb. I'd never really seen anyone with a beard. It wasn't like I grew up in New York; this was Minneapolis.

Later, when I was about fifteen and failing at school, my cousin took me to the Lubavitch house and there was the same guy who was the actor, this rabbi, Moshe Feller. He started talking and I said, "I don't want you to waste a lot of your time because, first of all, I don't believe in God, so let's just start there," figuring that that would end it.

"You don't believe in God," he said. "It's not a big deal. So put on *tefillin*."

He gave me a pair of old *tefillin* and I liked them. They were really something to me. It wasn't about planting trees in Israel or carpet for the *shul*. It had a certain relevance and, in some way, I compartmentalized the *tefillin* with things that were surreptitious in our home. The same place I would blow the pot out the basement window was the same place where I would put on the *tefillin*. It didn't really stick, though, because I didn't have any reinforcement. Later on, when I moved to New York with my band, I remember thinking, in retrospect, that it was odd that I took those *tefillin*.

Beverly: Little by little, once he went to New York, Peter became more involved with the Lubavitchers. In some ways, it was a good thing. It grounded him and gave him parameters. There's something about being on stage and everyone screaming about you. This kind of Judaism limits you. It creates boundaries and codifies your life, something that few people in the entertainment world have. On the other hand, it has limited his career, not being able to be with people and schmooze and make deals.

Peter: One day in New York, I got a phone call from these people for whom I'd writtten music for a teddy bear that's used in rape crisis, and so forth. The bear, ironically, is named Spinoza, heretic Jew. These two women told me that they just talked to a psychic and that I had only a few months to live. So I decided to meet with the psychics, a husband and wife team, and they were kind of . . . I guess they were normal as psychics go. "Is it your wish to leave the planet?" they asked. I heartily said no, and they seemed relieved. They said that I'd been doing music that was not necessarily true to my heart. My dad had died about a year before and I remember talking about him and this pain that was unexpressed. I remember feeling utterly frustrated. Then, out of the fog of confusion there came a little light on a train . . . the song I had written for my dad on his last Father's Day. Everyone had expected me to write a funny ditty to cheer my dad up but, instead, the song said everything that I wanted to say and I had cried at the end. It hit me: "Why don't I put out the song I wrote for my dad?"

I wound up putting out a whole record around it, with that being the title track. That record and video I made got me on MTV and got me my record deal. That was about the time I started going to Crown Heights. With the record deal, I got a bunch of money, which I'd never had before. I went to Israel. I bought *tefillin*. I went to the Wall. That's what I did with my first money.

The last show I ever played on *Shabbat* was when we opened for Joe Cocker in Cleveland. I'd met my wife and I saw a picture of how the future could be. I knew that if I had children, I didn't want to have the great so-called powers dictating which of my time was for sale. I needed to be in control.

Beverly: At first, when Peter became observant, I was very concerned. There were things he couldn't do with the family because there were all these rules. We had been a fairly tight-knit group and suddenly this came between us, and I felt like I was not good enough, not Jewish enough. I don't feel that way any longer. I'm Jewish the way I'm Jewish, and I'm plenty Jewish. I'm not kosher and don't keep *Shabbat*. I go to *shul* and I light *Shabbat* candles. With my women's group, we've developed our own rituals. I feel I'm as Jewish as anyone and I don't want to argue the point.

There's something wonderful, though, about celebrating *Shabbat* at Peter's house. There's a joy that you seldom see. It's a fun night, with so much anticipation. I love that they do it.

In some situations, sometimes I feel a little embarrassed. We used to rent a house in Del Mar, on the beach. In the morning, they'd go out on the patio in front to *daven* with the *tefillin* and tallises. They're *davening* and *shukeling* and I'm thinking, "Oh, my God." Last winter, my granddaughter came to visit and I needed to *kasher* the pans. We took two full Bloomingdale's shopping bags. We were standing knee-deep in the ocean, dipping the pans, and people were asking, "What the hell is she doing?" We laughed. It was sort of strange but fun.

Peter: My mom likes me so much and thinks I'm so great that she just doesn't care. She does what we need in terms of *kashrut*.

Beverly: My kids are my best friends. I'd do it for a friend; why wouldn't I do it for my kids? It's a real pain in the ass, but it's getting easier. I have more stuff in the house. Usually, I pride myself in setting a beautiful table but I sure can't do it when the kids are here. We have a lot of fun but my table looks like hell, with aluminum-foil pans.

I used to be a classroom teacher; we taught as a team. The classroom had to be as quiet overall as the least tolerant teacher wanted. It's the same with *kashrut*. If you're a family, you go along with the person who is the most conservative. The rest have to go along.

13

UP IN MY HEAD
Brent Baer

Jerusalem
December 17, 1991

Dear Mom and Dad,

I hope you are doing well and are in good health! It was so nice to talk with you the other night! I always enjoy our conversations and loved the Baer Cassette #2 and your recent letters.

Mom, you mentioned that you weren't quite sure "what I'm thinking up in my head." And, Dad, you shared from your heart your concerns with what I am doing and why I'm doing it. I didn't realize you felt so uncertain as to what I am doing. I know we've shared so much together; I thought you understood. Being sensitive, and now realizing you have uncomfortable questions in your minds, I will try to share with you what's "up in my head" in an effort to clarify for you my thinking and motivations.

I know that you have a vision for me: working, married, raising a family and living a healthy, happy life. I share that very same vision. It's a priority for me to earn a nice living and have a wonderful wife and children that we can all be proud of; it rings very deep within me! Dad, as you'd say, "I get it. Honest!"

It's of no surprise that in a Mishnah in *Gemara Kiddushin* describing fatherhood, it discusses that a father is supposed to help prepare his son for a profession and marry him off. Basically, it says that it is not appropriate for a son to retreat from the "real world" and not face responsibilities. I suppose you get your concerns, "Honest," as well. Both from my own emotions and the Jewish texts I'm learning from, you are right on target, and I'm thankful you've instilled those values within me.

So, if our goals are the same, what am I doing in Yeshiva Machon Shlomo?

First, I'm not taking the next thirty years of my life to learn how to become a monk. Rather, my yeshiva learning is a short-term program to improve the quality of my life and to enrich my future. I'm taking time, while I can, to deepen my level of self-knowledge, self-respect, and self-control, in addition to deepening my relationship with God and my understanding of and commitment to Judaism.

Second, we all recognize that I have natural talent and creative abilities: from winning talent shows, to receiving the Brazilian Fellowship and Top Business Student Award at George Washington University, to delivering presentations at International Marketing Association Conferences, to being the top worldwide salesperson at Dale Carnegie. Yet, with all the accomplishments, I've felt like a "microphone"—a good talker, but lacking real substance behind the microphone. It's time for substance.

I have the packaging, but without the depth. I portray a successful image in the world, but live with a type of existential vacuum inside. Success doesn't touch the deepest parts of a human being. It massages the ego and makes a man feel empowered and important. But success, alone, is superficial and lacking. Success doesn't penetrate man's essence and make him feel like he has purpose.

Third, there are some big, yet basic questions that I've just begun to relate to:

Why be good?

Why do some people have money and a nice family and still find life empty or lacking meaning?

Why go to shul?

What do the words of prayer mean? Speaking to God should not be boring, but uplifting.

What is my ultimate purpose?

Why do we give charity? How much should we contribute?

What obligations, if any, do I have as a Jew?

How have the Jews been able to survive for 3,000 years, and what does being "Jewish" mean?

You've always told me not to be gullible and just accept things, but to investigate thoroughly. That is exactly what I'm doing—digging deeper and deeper for the truth.

Fourth, you instilled within me the pride of being Jewish. Remember Donna? Donna and I at Rutgers? I went through a lot of pain breaking up with her. I didn't see your wisdom back then, but now it all makes perfect sense. Twelve years later, I can sincerely say thank you! You planted within me the seeds of Jewish identity. Now the tree is growing. The fruit of the tree is almost here; God willing, with my children (your grandchildren) to get nachas from. The Torah refers to sons as "builders." Accordingly, I want to take all you've given me and enhance it, add on to it. It's time for me to contribute in my own way. In effect, you passed me the baton and I'm now beginning to run the race.

Just as a seed that is planted in the dirt breaks apart and seemingly decays before the plant blooms, so too I have gone "undercover," working on and refining myself, so that I will bloom into a productive, happy leader, husband, father and citizen—a mensch.

It is true that during these months it appears from a distance that there is no growth, and time and money are slipping away. However, just as a seed needs to go underground to absorb necessary nutrients to survive as a future plant, I too am gaining the discipline, moral backbone, and spiritual underpinnings to help me shape my successful future.

The previous couple of generations slipped away from most Jewish observances yet retained the proud "feeling" of being Jewish. I don't think that Judaism can survive on a "feeling." I've made a decision to educate myself.

So, am I running away from reality? Am I being lazy? Am I wasting time? Am I being brainwashed?

The answer is . . . no.

I have taken a step of utmost strength and clarity in which I'm incorporating my upbringing, education, and skills. It's very satisfying to know what you're doing is right.

I am a Jew. I'm getting to know who I am in order

to live a fulfilling life of purpose and commitment to strong moral values.

I've already experienced growth in some key areas. The following lists a few involving self-control and education:

I wake up early, seven days a week.

I've kept my sense of humor, but no longer need to turn everything into a joke. I'm refining my sense of when to be serious and when to be light.

I've read more in the last year than in the last twenty years combined.

I'm thinking more clearly and being challenged and stimulated in a way I never thought possible.

I'm learning how to think, rigorously persevere, and come to conclusions.

I'm working on improving my character traits such as humility, tolerance, and chesed (kindness).

I want a deeper understanding of Judaism and want to practice Judaism as an adult, with an adult's level of knowledge. If I am a Jew, then I owe it to myself and to you to learn about who I am. Looking back on my life, I find it difficult to believe I let an eighteen-year-old child direct me on how to live the past thirteen years. I'm a thirty-year-old man and am committed to continuously improving the quality of my life.

I love you both deeply. I know you care about me and really want me to be happy! (Mom, all my friends comment about the Western Wall collage of photos. All the pictures and letters and concern keep me "going" here.)

You've been such good role models: family oriented, kind, demonstrating leadership and communication skills, committed to community development, thoughtful, and fair. I've come to appreciate the values you've given me and I'm grateful I've been able to incorporate many of them within me. I hope I can pass those on to my children.

I know that you trust me and respect me and will give me the rope I need to make my own life choices. I hope one day soon you will understand and get nachas from me and what I'm doing.

With love and respect,
Brent

14

JUDAISM
AS THE OTHER WOMAN
Gary Kornfeld

*M*y whole world came to a halt with the death of my first wife, Sharon. She was thirty-two years old and had struggled for two years with leukemia. To live so close to death for so long stirred something very deep inside me, something that had begun in the months leading up to her death. For the first time in my life, I was moved—forced to search, to ask, to seek an understanding for myself. Reciting the *Kaddish* prayer daily for a year forced me to confront my concept of God, of life, and of Judaism.

Without a wife and alone, I had plenty of time to take on this quest, to begin my journey. After some extensive research into various other concepts of God (Hindu, Buddhist, Muslim, and Christian), I realized that I first had to understand who I was and where I came from. The answer throughout my childhood—"We're special because we are Jews"—offered no meaning or solace. The Judaism of my childhood was more about "being Jewish" than Judaism. Jewish culture was a weak message on religion and God. The messengers forgot, diluted, and lost the message. Instead of walking away from God and Judaism, or turning inward with anger, I cried out to God for answers, for meaning, and for the truth of what Judaism had to offer me.

I discovered much beauty, wisdom, joy, and fulfillment in the heart and soul of Judaism. In time, study, prayer, and *Shabbat* came to replace things like golf, television, and football. This new "seriousness" in Gary, as many viewed it, was when things got sticky with my parents.

Two years after leaving the home I had shared with Sharon to begin a "new" life in another state, I decided to open a kosher deli, a *glatt* kosher deli that was closed on *Shabbat*. My father thought I was crazy. His world is dollars and cents, and he thought the decision to close on *Shabbat* was ridiculous. He was convinced that my beliefs would destroy me financially. And when the deli closed after a year, it was the stamp of approval on his beliefs. "Get some balance and get away from that Judaism," were his words.

Had I been successful financially, my father's attitudes may have been different. He was judging Judaism by what he saw as a poor business choice. Judaism was the culprit, the "other woman," the thing to blame.

The deli was a dream that lived, that drew in community and affected many people's lives. The night I closed the doors, just before *Shabbat*, was the same night that my new wife, Deb, and I conceived our first child.

When the door to one dream closes, another one opens. I hope my parents will grow to respect my choices. I want to teach my daughter to respect her grandparents and, at the same time, value our observant life.

15

FAQs PEOPLE ASKED
WHEN I MARRIED AN
ORTHODOX MAN
Rita Schwartz Singer

I was raised Jewish style. We ate matzoh and lit Chanukah candles at the appropriate times, but Judaism wasn't a big part of our lives. I'm from New York where everyone eats bagels and lox.

I got more interested in Judaism, visited Israel, met a nice Jewish man. We had so much in common that he understood my jokes. We had big differences, too, such as his kids were little, my daughter was grown up. Such as I'm very tidy and he's definitely not tidy. And he's a *ba'al teshuvah*—a newly Orthodox person.

He asked me to marry him and I couldn't resist. I promised to be observant.

Oy Veh! You'd think I was marrying a Martian.

FREQUENTLY ASKED QUESTIONS
FROM FRIENDS, FAMILY,
AND PERFECT STRANGERS

Question: Don't you miss eating lobster (bacon, cheese-burgers, spareribs)?

Answer: Yep, but they're so high in cholesterol. (*And now I get my cholesterol from* kasha, kishka, *and* knaydlach.)

Question: How can you cook all that heavy food?

Answer: He does the cooking. (*I should learn how, but why ruin a good thing?*)

Question: Will your husband make your quit your job?

Answer: Why would he want to? (*He can't* make *me do* anything.)

Question: Will your husband let you play poker?

Answer: He doesn't *let* me do anything. (*Especially when I'm on a winning streak.*)

Question: Isn't it embarrassing (weird, dangerous) that he wears a *kipa*?

Answer: No, he's making a statement that he's a Jew. (*It beats that John Deere cap.*)

Question: Will you have to wear frumpy clothes?

Answer: Scarves, flowing skirts, modesty in a tacky world. *Frum,* not frumpy. (*The sight of my bare legs is not such a thrill.*)

Question: How can you give up Friday nights and Saturdays?

Answer: We spend *Shabbos* unplugged with friends and family. It's fabulous. (*How did I ever manage without* Shabbos *naps?*)

Question: Do you have to shave your head (walk ten paces behind your husband, stop using deodorant)?

Answer: No, where do rumors like that get started? (*Good grief, where do rumors like that get started?*)

Question: What if I want to talk to you on Saturday?

Answer: Come over. (*Have some chicken soup, sit a while.*)

Question: Isn't it weird not to have sex for two weeks each month (to go to the *mikveh,* to wait till you're married to have sex)?

Answer: Yep, and we never take sex for granted. (*Abstinence is shockingly erotic.*)

Question: So they're converting you, too?

Answer: Ma, we've always been Jewish.

16

A LOT TO SWALLOW
Alan Perlman

Dear Mom,

Last weekend was certainly an unusual weekend for our family. These days it seems as though any weekend that I am able to take leave from my very hectic work schedule and come home is somewhat unusual. However, my latest visit was unusually unusual. For the first time, the family seemed to truly become aware of what I have been spending much of the last three years doing and experiencing. I can imagine that through your eyes, my last three years' exploration into Judaism was, in many ways, simply an extension of my living in England. As both living in England and living an observant Jewish lifestyle were not part of our common family history, the reality of the existence of each in my life could only be perceived in the abstract. While the family was exposed in my previous trips of my desire to observe Shabbos, this latest trip underscored how Judaism has become much more central in my entire life and not just "one day out" of the week. I know how surprising this has been for everyone.

I have always had a great deal of pride in the extraordinary closeness we have as a family. We clearly have an exceptional amount of love, respect, and concern for one another. I am certain that this degree of closeness will never be in jeopardy. Not with you. Nor with Kari and Mike. And not with Dad. You are all sources of strength for me. The family's love and support has been invaluable in my past successes and will no doubt be invaluable in my future goals. I hope that I have demonstrated similar love and support as well.

I am very appreciative of your efforts to make last weekend a success. You went above and beyond the call of duty in attempting to provide for a strictly kosher meal at home without any prior experience, supplies, and awareness of what foods are considered "kosher." This was even more impressive given that much of your preparation occurred on Shabbos, preventing you from consulting with anyone who had prior experience in this realm. It certainly did not help matters that the entire meal was thrust upon you with little time to prepare. To complicate matters further, you had to accomplish this task knowing that my guest at the meal, whom you would be meeting for the first time, was a potential daughter-in-law. It certainly wasn't just the kosher food that was a lot to swallow.

For many of my thirty-one years, I have been preoccupied with deriving meaning from my life. Where did this preoccupation come from? Perhaps the seeds of this desire stem from my experience as an eleven-year-old witnessing the two people whom I most loved separate from one another. Perhaps these seeds were planted even earlier by childhood recollections of witnessing a cancer-stricken grandmother in her final years of life, or maybe it stems from the ever-perpetual struggle in our family to make financial ends meet. After much reflection, I think that it is more likely that the real roots of this desire stem from your instruction. You have always emphasized to me the importance of deriving the most from my life's experiences. Your encouragement to pursue a bar mitzvah (despite the competing pressures of football and baseball practice) is a clear example. The same follows for your encouragement to pursue a career choice that provides meaning in an occupation rather than one that only emphasizes financial security. Even my trips to Europe, Costa Rica, Israel, and Africa had ties to this encouragement, as they are clearly reflective of a philosophy of using diverse experiences as one vehicle to maximize meaning from life. My exploration into Judaism is a by-product of this emphasis on deriving meaning from life.

Mom, as I continue to search for meaning in my life, there will always be certain constants for me that will never change, despite how dramatic my recent lifestyle modifications seem to appear at present. The greatest and most significant constant is the profound love and respect that I have for our family. I have always been thankful of the family that I have inherited. You, in particular, have illustrated for me the importance of family values, sensitivity, compassion, giving, and kindness. These five traits are central goals for my own personal development, as well as traits that I am searching for in a marriage partner. I hope to eventually instill these traits within my own family. It is my desire that my future spouse and children will be able to witness firsthand these characteristics that you possess, as well as our exceptional closeness as a group. It would disappoint me greatly if Judaism resulted in your feeling excluded from my life. I know that currently my involvement in Judaism seems to offer nothing but barriers to our family dynamics. However, from my personal experience over the last three years, I can honestly say that one major by-product of a Jewish lifestyle is the centrality of family. Fortunately, Judaism does offer the flexibility to make most conceivable family circumstances workable, and I do not see why this would be any different for our family. You must understand that this is one of my goals.

You are very special to me and I love you very much.

Love,
Alan

17

GRABBING A MITZVAH
Yosef Branse

When I began studying at a yeshiva in Jerusalem and informed my parents that I was becoming observant, my father wrote to me: "The one thing a son of mine could do that would hurt me the most would be to become religious." This hardly bode well for the maintenance of stable relations between me and my parents in my new situation.

Yet, in the years that followed, there were very few words of open rebuke, never any break in the lines of communication. I had severely disappointed my parents by my incomprehensible break with the course of my life till then (after earning my B.A. degree, I had immediately found a good job, which I gave up after less than two years in order to backpack around Europe).

My parents fully expected me to return at the end of

the *wanderjahr* and resume the thread of professional life. Exactly what profession wasn't entirely clear to any of us, and it didn't really matter.

Besides the shattering of his dreams for my personal satisfaction, my religious turn irritated my father as an affront to his atheism. He had had no substantial Jewish education in his youth. His attitudes toward religion were shaped, I believe, by the smug dismissal it received in academic and scientific circles in the postwar world confident that technological progress would be the salvation of humanity.

He would sometimes expound his belief in how primitive humanity had come to invent God, in response to primeval fears of natural forces. I suspect he absorbed that approach in some college course.

But in fact, debates about religion were few and far between. We observed a long, unwritten truce on the subject. Less than a year after my return to America, I returned to Israel for good, married and started raising my family. Distance blurred the ideological differences, and longing for grandchildren seen only at too-long intervals overshadowed objections to the lifestyle in which they were raised. When we visited my parents in America, kosher foods and one-time utensils were available in abundance, and the household was adapted as necessary for *Shabbat* observance.

On my parents' visits to our home in the development town of Migdal haEmek, the truce held. One year their visit coincided with Sukkot. Although climbing and descending stairs was difficult for my father, he negotiated the frequent two-flight descent from our apartment to the *sukkah*, and the corresponding upstairs trek, without complaint. I know he was not comfortable and would much rather have remained in the apartment, but he made the effort for the sake of *shalom bayit*.

I am not sure that I was so accommodating. I recall

one incident in which my young son, while staging an impressive tantrum in the hallway by the entrance to our apartment, chucked his *kipa*. I would not let him in until he retrieved it. "I don't want him in the house without a *kipa!*" I shouted. Later, I wondered whether my bare-headed father, standing nearby, had sensed some subliminal message in my words.

In the summer of 1992, I traveled to Florida with my three oldest children, all boys, at my parents' invitation. We traveled to Disney World and other tourist attractions and visited with relatives. For the boys, it was a dream vacation and I, despite my misgivings about the risks the venture posed to their religious worldview, had a good time also.

One day we visited an elderly aunt, who was in her late eighties. After I described to her our community of American immigrants in Migdal haEmek, and the educational system we maintained, she commented: "You know, I have a friend here who every year donates $1,000 to a different place in Israel. Maybe she'd like to contribute to your school." She arranged a meeting with the lady, who was quite happy to see my young sons with their *kipot* and *peot*.

At the end of our get-together, and without any pleading on my part, the kind lady wrote out a check for $1,000 to the educational institutions of our *kehilla*.

As luck would have it, another member of our community was in the United States at the same time, raising funds in the New York area. I called him up and asked what we should do with the money. He told me to send it to him at the address where he was staying.

The next day, my father drove me to the post office and I mailed the check. Afterward, I felt a twinge of concern; perhaps I should have sent it registered mail? My father reassured me that it would be all right. He had sent larger amounts by regular mail, he said, and nothing ever went astray.

Soon afterward, my boys and I returned to Israel, laden with presents and happy memories. Some time later, we got a call from the *shaliach's* wife, relaying a question from her husband, who was still in New York: Where was the check? I began to worry. The money should have arrived by then. I chastised myself for not sending such a considerable sum by registered mail.

More time went by, with no sign of the check. The *shaliach* returned to Israel. What should we do? Just write it off? Our school could not afford to pass by such a generous donation just because of some slip-up in the postal service.

I called my father and asked him to assist. Of course, this meant approaching the donor, explaining the situation, and asking for a new check. This was no easy feat. The nursing home where my aunt and her friend lived was quite a distance from my parents' home, at least half an hour by car. Furthermore, the lady was not easy to deal with, due to hearing loss and other infirmities as a result of her advanced age.

I can well imagine what a chore it must have been, but my father saw it through. After several months of contacts and waiting for the outcome of bank inquiries, it turned out that the check had been cashed, using a forged endorsement. We will never know where it was intercepted, nor by whom, but the bank acknowledged that it had been honored improperly and reimbursed the donor's account. She then wrote a new check, which my father sent to us in Israel—via registered mail, of course.

I know that that mission was no easy feat for my father. He was sixty-eight years old at the time and not in the best of health. More than the physical and emotional drain it must have been on him, I have always wondered about the irony of the situation in which this self-proclaimed atheist invested time and effort to retrieve money for an ultra-Orthodox school so much the antithesis of his intellectual beliefs.

He could have just shrugged the whole thing off, as it was clearly none of his responsibility. He could have told us to deal with the matter by phone from Israel, which would have meant, in effect, dooming any prospect of retrieving the donation. Instead, without any cajoling, he took upon himself to be a *shaliach mitzvah*.

I never asked him why, nor did I have much opportunity. The last time I saw him was in 1994, when my parents came to Israel for my eldest son's bar mitzvah. He died suddenly in January 1996.

I like to believe, though I can't prove it, that my father's efforts were an expression of the *pintele Yid* present in every Jew, no matter how estranged from his roots. This was a means of "grabbing a *mitzvah*" in his twilight years, laying in a supply of merits while there was still time. Outwardly, nothing changed in his attitude toward Judaism and religion in general, and I have no firm evidence that anything had changed inwardly either.

Perhaps there is a lesson for us in this. Chazal (the rabbis of the Talmud) say that when a *mitzvah* comes your way, don't pass it up. The world presents us with endless opportunities for *gemilut chasadim* (acts of lovingkindness); sometimes they are right under our noses, but we are not sensitive enough to go after them. My father may not have been consciously aware of the *mitzvah* he was performing, and he was probably indifferent to the idea of being rewarded for it in the next world. Nonetheless, instead of shirking from the opportunity that came his way, he gave it his best efforts.

How much more should people who perform *mitzvot* from conviction try to be aware of the chances that come our way, and not slacken in our determination to fulfill them to the best of our abilities.

Part III

The Rabbis Speak

INTRODUCTION

*F*or many non-observant parents, the boogeyman wears a *kipa* and is called "Rebbe." The phrase, "my rebbe says," strikes fear in the secular heart as it is generally followed by yet another restriction, yet another way in which everyone's life is going to change.

The rabbis are often seen as the ultimate puppeteers, pulling the strings that move children away from the secular world in which they grew up. Some parents see these rabbis as wardens of some bizarre halachic prison. One *ba'al teshuvah* tells of an incident that occurred shortly after he had informed his parents of his decision to keep kosher. He arrived for dinner at his parents' house only to discover that his mother was serving shrimp cocktail. "But, Mom," said the *ba'al teshuvah*, "I told you that I am now keeping kosher." His mother replied simply, "That's why I thought this would be a special treat."

Yet many rabbis, especially those featured in this section, have themselves embarked on a spiritual journey. They, too, are often at odds with their families. They, too, have struggled to find their balance.

Rabbi David Teutsch, the president of the Reconstructionist Rabbinical College in Pennsylvania, remembers an incident that occurred when he was in college, after he had stopped eating pork but before he stopped eating all non-kosher meat. "I was visiting a relative in Germany, a man who had been part of the underground during the war and was never captured. In those days, my German was pretty good. When dinner was served, it didn't look like any meat that I recognized. When I asked my cousin what it was, he said that it was lamb. I believed him, since my general way of working in the world is to take people's statements at face value. When the food had been cleared from the table, my cousin told me with great delight that the meat was, in fact, a pork roast. He laughed and said that I should see from the fact that I was healthy that my views were superstitious."

Teutsch goes on to explain that "the easiest thing to do when you've had an experience like that is to draw into your own little world and associate only with people like yourself. Yet, that is terribly counterproductive. *Kashrut* is supposed to be a system that reminds us to be attentive to the extraordinary gift of the food we eat. It's meant to heighten our respect for animal life and make us conscious of the importance of acts connected to food but, in my mind, it's not meant to set up barriers between Jews. For me, the question is how do we embrace those observances that can carry great meaning without building barriers between people?"

Rabbi Zalman M. Schachter-Shalomi starts off this section, describing his journey from a Lubavitcher yeshiva to an eco-kosher kitchen. Rabbi Allen Selis explains how Jews have become like *goyim* to one another. In a very thoughtful interview, Rabbi Joel Lehrfield explains that American secular Jews, the parents of the *ba'alei teshuvah*, have difficulty understanding their children's acceptance of the concept of a divine, immutable law. Then, using a story from Rabbi Nachman of Bratslav, Rabbi Shlomo Porter shows how non-observant parents can embrace observant practices without changing their identity.

Rabbi Robert Schreibman believes that non-observant relatives must take the first steps of compromise toward their more observant family members. Next, in a letter to his children, Rabbi Robert Dobrusin tells about his Uncle Simcha, a *tzaddik* who traveled with a plate and a hard-boiled egg, so he could eat with those who did not observe as he did. Rabbi Doug Weber uses Jesus' words to express his concern that some *mitzvot*, like *kashrut* and *Shabbat* observance, have been elevated above other *mitzvot*.

Rabbi Shlomo Riskin describes the *Shabbat* afternoon when his non-observant mother wondered if God had made a mistake putting her together with a "religious" son. Rabbi Mordecai Twerski emphasizes how important it is for the rabbi to be a facilitator of communication between the newly observant and their families. Finally, Rabbi Amy Wallk Katz describes being caught between a rock and a hard place—non-observant in-laws and a brother who won't eat in her home.

18

SHARP HORSERADISH
Rabbi Zalman M. Schachter-Shalomi

A long time ago, for me at least—to be precise it was in 1943—when I was studying at the Lubavitcher Yeshivah in Brooklyn, we used to say to each other, "*L'Chayim.* May you have children who won't eat in your house because they will be more *frum* (observant) than you." And we considered this a blessing.

Today this blessing has been fulfilled for me and I want to say, "*Barukh HaShem!*" Thank God. My daughter, now married to a Bratzlaver Hassid and living in Jerusalem, when she last visited needed to be served food especially prepared and served to meet her standard.

Does this make me happy? Well, yes, like sharp horseradish on fish. Certainly not like a sweet *lokshen kugel* (noodle pudding).

I deserve this, as one says in Yiddish, *Ich hob zikh dos*

kosher un heilig Fardihnt. I did the same to my parents—not drinking the milk without a kosher certification and each *Pesach* not eating *gebrocht* (meaning any form of matzah that came in contact with water). *Knaidlakh* (matzoh balls) were a no-no for me. Now I am more concerned with organic and eco-kosher, with a company's labor practices and fair trade, than with a certification on a product.

The family counseling situations that I have been involved in have ranged from those in which parents considered engaging cult deprogrammers to those who feared that they would lose their children to those who suddenly felt tyrannized by their kids. I bless the parents who will have patience and value the connection with their now "estranged" children more than their inconvenience and their ego. It may turn out that the parents who first humor their children and bring *kashrut* into their homes will get the hang of it. They may appreciate *Shabbat* for the emancipation it offers from the stress of the shopping mall/office and work strain and enjoy the singing of *zmirot* (songs of praise) and the value of talk around the Sabbath table.

And perhaps the children who experience the parents' acceptance of them in their new lifestyle will, after a while, come to appreciate their parents' balanced life and embrace it.

So what if the children insist on a *hechsher* and paper plates when they eat at their parents' home? It only interferes with the parents' expectations and habit of being boss in the house. I would rather have the kids at home and feeling at home when they come than be "right."

19

HOW FAR TO BEND?
Rabbi Allen Selis

*I*n Chapter 12 of the book of Exodus, the Torah goes into explicit detail regarding the laws of Passover. In presenting the restriction against eating raised or fermented products during the week of Passover, the Torah notes: "No leaven food shall be found in your houses for seven days. Whoever eats anything that is leaven shall be cut off from the community of the house of Israel. . . ." (Exodus 12:19) For years, this verse has rung in my ears with terrible irony. In my life, the verse operates in reverse. I'm the one who keeps kosher, yet it is I who often feel cut off from my family and my community.

The dietary dissonance follows me from place to place, from event to event. At a Mother's Day brunch, my grandmother whisks away a dish of seafood sauce before I can ladle it onto my salmon. "Not for you," she says, "that's the sauce we put on the crab cakes." At Thanksgiving, we usher visiting relatives into town. On the first of several excursions to local restaurants, I am nuzzled between calamari on one side, and chicken parmigiana on the other. Worst of all was the family gathering some years ago. At a packed table of parents, grandparents, and cousins, my plate was the only one that lacked for shrimp. I sat watching my family enjoy their seafood and felt myself draw further and further away from the relatives who sat around me. Who are these people, and what do we have in common? What values of mine do they share? I scowled through dinner over my pasta primavera, feeling more and more like an unwanted, unwelcome guest.

In the Talmud, the rabbis discuss the *kashrut* of a number of foods made by idolatrous pagans. The foods are all essentially kosher: wine, oil, bread, and the like. They could not have been distinguished in any way from the oil or bread that a Jew might press or bake. But the rabbis forbade other Jews to eat these foods if they were prepared by non-Jews. The reason that the rabbis offered is curt and to the point: "weddings." If Jews were allowed to eat in the same places as non-Jews, they would fall into conversation, build fellowship, and ultimately come to marry one another. A big no-no. So, hoping to avoid this, the rabbis employed the dietary laws as a tool for creating social separation. The message conveyed by the statement, "I can't eat your food," is essentially to say that "you are fundamentally different. Our travels might intersect, but we don't share the same path. You stay on yours. I'll stay on mine." The rabbis who originally promulgated this ruling, some two millennia ago, would be shocked to see how common it is that Jewish parents and children cannot eat at one another's tables. We have become like *goyim* to one another.

How to bridge the gap? Eating is a fundamental part

of social connection, as the rabbis understood so well. If I cannot eat together with others, I really am conveying the message that they do not fit into my life. Over the years, I have seen my own observance of *kashrut* play back and forth between the standards that I observe while eating alone, and those that I follow while joining others. I have never eaten anything that I could not defend as 100% kosher, but let's just say that I have found a time and a place for the "gold" standard of *kashrut,* as opposed to the "silver" or "copper" standard. Perhaps at a family gathering I won't be so picky about the plates, the spoons, or which *hechsher* is on the chocolate. The food is not the issue. What matters is that I will go out of my way to eat with people for whom I care. Sometimes I regret the stretch. But more often than not, it's worthwhile. So once in a while, *kashrut* gets turned on its head. Instead of reminding me who I should stay away from, my extra work to keep kosher with non-kosher friends and family reminds me that there is a religious imperative towards maintaining positive human connections.

My best experience of such stretching goes back to April of 1990. It was the first time since I had begun to keep kosher that I spent Passover with my decidedly non-kosher family. The negotiations began weeks in advance. One oven would be meticulously scrubbed and self-cleaned. My aunt purchased new boxes of plastic silverware and paper napkins. I *kashered* one pot to prepare the hard-boiled eggs. We bought one new knife, one new bowl, and a cutting board to prepare the charoset, the vegetables, and anything else that might go into my mouth that evening. And finally, the *coup de grace*: The hosts of the Seder proffered one single, foil-wrapped serving of strictly kosher-for-Passover turkey breast and double-stuffed potatoes, straight from Pikesville's best-known kosher caterer. At the same time, I did not pay too much attention to the forbidden foods on anyone else's plate. I did my thing. My family did theirs. And somehow, we all managed to share the same table that evening. In the end, what I remember least about the evening is the food. What I remember most is the joy of sharing an evening of celebration with my family. For all of us, it was worth the stretch.

20

NOT EQUALS
Rabbi Joel Lehrfield

Question: Why do some parents have so much difficulty with the structure of the observant life their child has chosen?

Answer: For most American Jews, religion is not an imperative and a *mitzvah* is not a commandment. Instead, a *mitzvah* is perceived as merely a good deed. As, I believe, Ted Koppel once said, the Ten Commandments have become the Ten Suggestions. For the Orthodox, however, a *mitzvah* remains an imperative, part of the divinely ordained Torah. This comment brings me to my next point.

As Americans, we view the law as man-made. Democratically appointed representatives write laws, hopefully for the benefit of their citizenry. At the same time, they have the right to repeal or change the laws they write. The whole idea of a divine, God-given, immutable law is foreign to most American Jews. The Achilles' heel, therefore, in terms of compromise, is that we think we are dealing with two equals and we are not. We cannot co-opt divine law and treat it as equal to man-made law. This concept of divine law is very difficult for non-observant parents to understand. They understand the concept of law in a civil/criminal sense, but they cannot comprehend the idea of a religiously mandated law.

I suspect that in place of a prevailing view on what Judaism is, most American Jews do not hold fast to a particularly cohesive religious position. For a cohesive, cognate position they substitute an attitude or feeling. If there is any kind of position taken, it is: "No one can tell me what to do." Hence, the notion that "Our Father, Our King" commands us to eat or not to eat certain substances falls on if not rebellious, then certainly deaf, ears. And so the generations fail to hear what the other has to say.

Question:　Can parents expect compromise as a form of respect for the family?

Answer:　When there is conflict in a family, there is often the expectation that family peace, *shalom bayit*, is the paramount value and should prevail. To ask the question "What does *HaShem* really want from us?" is to introduce, for less observant parents, an irrelevant question. If God is a less important element and we substitute "family" as the chief good, we are really displacing *HaShem* from his throne. Isn't that a form of idolatry? It is no different than substituting any other good (e.g. money, power, health, and so forth) for God. Anything standing in the way of our commitment to God and Torah and viewed as a superior value is idolatrous. The rabbis, in an interesting comment to just such a question as described, raise the rhetorical question as to which opinion is superior, the teacher or his student. If God is the teacher, and parents are his students, then it is apparent whose law will be followed and observed. For the Jew who is committed to the idea that we are a unique community serving a unique purpose, he or she cannot act traitorously to God.

Question: How does a family begin to resolve their conflicts?

Answer: Oftentimes, from a psychological perspective, religion becomes the arena of conflict when, in fact, it is not the source of the conflict. It is relatively easy to blame religion when the issues are much deeper and contain seeds of disappointments, hopes that weren't achieved, a sense of guilt, or the need to justify a position. Parents take their child's religious commitment as a personal affront. Religion and the issue of respect then become the safe ground from which war is waged.

Children have an obligation to accept their parents for who they are. The Torah doesn't ask you to love your parents; it commands you to respect them. In turn, an observant child should not be treated any less than the head of a foreign community. Each should offer the other, at the minimum, the civility and kindness they would offer a stranger, without the ego-driven needs that separate loved ones.

21

BE A TURKEY
BUT ACT LIKE A JEW
A Conversation with
Rabbi Shlomo Porter

*R*abbi Shlomo Porter, an Orthodox rabbi in Baltimore and president of the Association of Jewish Outreach Professionals, ran a support group several years ago. It was called Parents of Religious Children (PORC). Although the group no longer meets, Rabbi Porter counsels *ba'alei teshuvah* and their families.

"The story I tell parents is a parable of Rabbi Nachman of Bratslav," says Porter. "It's called 'The Turkey Prince.'"

"The Turkey Prince" is the tale of a young prince who one day decides that he is a turkey. He takes off his clothes, sits under the table, and pecks away at the crumbs on the floor. The king, distraught, asks for the assistance of all the royal physicians but, alas, no one can cure the prince.

One day a sage comes to the king and says he will try to cure the prince. The king agrees and the sage undresses, sits down on the floor with the prince, and he, too, starts pecking at the crumbs.

"Who are you?" asks the prince.

"I'm a turkey," replies the sage.

The prince and the sage stay together for some time and become friends. One day, the sage tells the king's servants to throw him shirts. The sage puts on a shirt and when the prince asks him what he's doing, the sage says, "Why do you think that a turkey cannot wear a shirt? You can wear a shirt and still be a turkey." So, the prince also puts on a shirt.

The sage beckons the servants again, this time asking for pants. Just as before, the sage and prince don the pants. This continues until both men are completely dressed. The sage then explains to the prince that he will still be a turkey even if he eats good food or sits at the table. And pretty soon the prince is completely cured.

When Rabbi Porter uses this parable with parents, he is making the point that parents do not need to change their identity. "There is no law in Reform Judaism that says you can't keep kosher," says Porter. "Don't change your identity; just do the action. You're keeping kosher not because of anything you believe. If your son said, 'I only eat Chinese,' you'd serve him Chinese. The real problem is the sense of judgment—'I'm not good enough, I don't keep kosher enough.' Parents feel it's a statement about themselves and it's not."

Porter also suggests that the *ba'alei teshuvah* have a responsibility to thank their parents. It's important to say words like, "I took you seriously when you told me that being a Jew is important. I built upon the principles you set down. You are the most important people in my life. You are my parents."

22

FOR THE SAKE OF PEACE
Rabbi Robert Schreibman

*I*n the Torah portion *Vayera,* more specifically Genesis 18:12, Sarah laughs when God tells her that she and Abraham will have a child. How is that possible when both she and her husband are so old, she wonders? When God repeats this conversation to Abraham, He says that Sarah laughed because she wondered how she could bear a child at her age. Conveniently left out is that Sarah laughed, as well, at the thought of Abraham becoming a father at his age.

The commentators are quick to point out that this discrepancy in the biblical text is done to prevent an argument between husband and wife, and is referred to as *shalom bayit,* "for the sake of peace." We find, in *Sefer Agadah,* that even the Holy One, Blessed be He, changes

His words to emphasize the importance of family harmony.

As a rabbi of some forty years, twenty-five of them at a liberal Reform Congregation on the North Shore of Chicago, I have heard stories of how the concept of *shalom bayit* is threatened when someone in the family insists on *kashrut*. In fact, this simple and pious act seems to be of greater nuisance and disturbance than becoming Orthodox itself.

Usually the decision to keep kosher is part of meticulously observing *halachah*, Jewish law. *Halachah* is believed by observant Orthodox Jews as divinely revealed. Thus, *halachah* must be fulfilled in its entirety by all Jews as the standard to live up to and by. It cannot be changed by whim or convenience. It is God's word!

Therefore, *shalom bayit* appears, at first glance, to be something that only a less observant Jew can observe, as the observant Jew cannot since it would mean disobedience to Divine dicta.

I have spoken with many families who have faced and tried to resolve this new phenomenon of orthodoxy in their lives. Their reactions have ranged from anger and disbelief to semi-acceptance. One parent said that she felt "skewered and is still squirming." Some parents felt that they had been "inadequate Jewish parents." A mother said she was angry with Judaism for "taking her son away." All had to examine their own attitudes and practices to see if they could adjust to something out of their control.

Some of the families sat down together to find out if things could be ironed out and to find out just what was going on. At the very least, this acted as a catharsis and began the tenuous road to healing. Even as family relationships became strained, attempts were made to create an environment where everyone felt as comfortable as possible. Since it is always easier for the less observant family to compromise, this is where it has to begin. The religious beliefs of the kosher relations mean more to those keeping kosher than any food could mean to the non-kosher since "food is food."

The first steps are compromises on the part of the non-kosher relatives; after all, "it is not a big deal to eat a turkey sandwich without cheese." Kosher deli trays, paper plates, and plastic utensils become *de rigeur*. One family in my experience would pay for the entire family to go to a *glatt* kosher hotel of the son's choosing for Seder. Another family turned their wet bar area into a separate kitchen for their son so that he could eat at home.

As the less observant family readjusts its own family rituals for the sake of *shalom bayit*, the strictly observant often try to become more flexible as well. Paper plates often give way to dishes. Some will even eat at the same table whether all the food is kosher or not. On occasion, newly observant Jews will allow family members to drive to their homes in order to observe *Shabbat* together.

My advice is to try to remain close, to show that everyone is loved and a valuable member of the family, and even if not reconciled with the choice, to show respect. Not only does this allow interaction to continue, it has other benefits for the newly observant. He or she can become a resource of religious advice and broadening the knowledge of Judaism for the whole family.

I believe that most Orthodox Jews believe in the concept of *shalom bayit* as strongly as non-Orthodox Jews. Obviously, it is more difficult for them to make any concessions at all, but generally they will try to make some accommodation when they see their less observant family show respect, love, and caring by their much more extensive compromises.

23

UNCLE SIMCHA'S MEAL
A letter
by Rabbi Robert Dobrusin
to his children

My dear children:

I want to tell you about a member of your family. His name was Simcha and he was your great-great-uncle. You don't remember him. He died many, many years ago.

The truth is that I don't remember him very well at all. He died when I was about five or six. One of the two things I do remember about him was that he died just before Kol Nidre services. He was all dressed for *shul* and sat down in his chair and died just before Yom Kippur began. Later, I learned that our tradition says that this type of death is reserved for *tzadikkim*, for righteous people. In this case, the tradition is right on target.

I say that because the only other thing I remember about him was how he used to come to visit our house for a family dinner. His actions at those dinners reflected righteousness.

Uncle Simcha would come in and sit down at the end of the table. He would open up a bag and take a tin plate he had brought from his home. He would reach into his pocket and pull out a hard-boiled egg and a packet of salt and eat with the family. He didn't say a word about what everyone else was eating. He just ate his hard-boiled egg and sat with the family.

He knew we didn't keep kosher and he wouldn't eat our food or eat off our plates. But, he wouldn't miss out on the family and wouldn't ask anyone to make any special arrangements. He just brought his hard-boiled egg and sat down and ate with the rest of us.

He taught me two things. He taught me how important *kashrut* was to him and how important family was to him. In his quiet way, he sent a very clear message. That, my children, was a *tzaddik*.

Now, let me tell you a story about a person you know better.

When I was about ten years old, our family began keeping kosher at home. Five years later, I decided to begin to keep kosher outside of the house as well. Shortly after I made this decision, we were invited for dinner to the home of a dear family friend. Her husband had recently died and she wanted us to come over for a summer barbecue, just as we had done for so many years.

I was presented with a dilemma. No doubt she would serve chicken. She always did. She did not observe *kashrut*. That had never bothered me before. But, it did now.

After some serious thought, I decided to eat chicken in her non-kosher home. After all, I reasoned, I hadn't yet told her of my decision to keep kosher outside the home and her husband had just died, and it wasn't nice to insult her and it would make the family happy.

That was a nice thing to do. In some ways, it was a very *mentschlicht* thing to do. But, thirty years later, I can tell you that it was not the right thing to do. I should have learned from Uncle Simcha and just quietly eaten the salad.

You see, my children, we all have our priorities. Being nice and kind is one priority we should all have. But, we can be nice and kind and respectful and thoughtful and still be loyal to our own commitments.

It was so right for me to care about her feelings and so wrong of me not to respect my own decisions.

In *kashrut*, and in other areas, balancing our own self-respect with kindness to others is sometimes very difficult. We each observe *kashrut* in our own way. While the laws of *kashrut* are clear, there are many issues that are custom, not law. There are many traditions that are not universally shared. Many of us choose to follow leniencies or strictures in certain areas. *Kashrut* is not an absolute, black-and-white issue. There are many, many gray areas and each of us makes our own decisions.

As you grow, you will make your decision about the way that we have observed *kashrut* and you will decide whether it's right or wrong for you. You will decide whether we have been too strict or too lenient or whether *kashrut* will mean anything to you at all.

I hope *kashrut* will always be meaningful to you and you will find the approach to *kashrut* with which you are comfortable. I don't expect that you'll do exactly what we do. You must find your own way. All I do ask is that you will remember the lessons that Uncle Simcha and I have taught you.

If you decide to be more lenient about *kashrut*, we will respect your right and won't make unreasonable requests. However, I won't compromise my deeply held principles just to "be nice." And, although disappointed, I will respect your right to live as you choose and will not make it an issue between us.

If you decide to be more strict about *kashrut*, you don't necessarily have to bring your own plate and egg to our house. We'll do what we can to make you comfortable. Just ask. But, if whatever we do isn't enough, and it may very well not be, remember Uncle Simcha and please don't make a *megillah* about it. Just come in with a smile and a kiss and a hug and eat whatever it is you can eat and sit at our table with us. Please don't ever make it an issue between us. Observe as you see fit, but always do it with respect for us and we will respect you in turn.

No one should ever have to compromise something they believe in deeply for some vague principle of "proper behavior." But, no one should allow something as important as "proper behavior" to be forgotten in the zeal to observe the *mitzvot*. Maybe you can't always be a *tzaddik* like Uncle Simcha, but you can always be a *mensch*.

Love,
Dad

24

THE MOUTH
IS A TWO-WAY STREET
Rabbi Doug Weber

*Then Jesus called the crowd to him and said to them,
"Listen and understand! It is not what goes into a person's
mouth that makes him ritually unclean; rather, what
comes out of it makes him unclean." (Matthew, 15:10–11
with parallel in Mark 7:14–15, Good News Bible:
Today's English Version)*

Two thousand years ago, Jesus of Nazareth ad-
dressed the never-ending issue: Do the "moral" laws of
the Torah supercede the "ritual" laws? His comment,
quoted in Matthew, is evidence of a first-century debate
about keeping kosher and its importance relative to the
other *mitzvot*.

Many Jews are surprised to learn that the Christian
Scriptures can shed light on the wide varieties of Judaism

that existed in the first century of the Common Era. We
learn much about ourselves by how outsiders perceive us.
Even when highly distorted and polemical, the Gospel
accounts depict certain tensions present in first-century
Judaism, some of which are not only alive today but are at
the heart of this book.

Jesus' words in Matthew (with a parallel in Mark)
are, according to a consensus of "historical Jesus" acade-
micians, among the more reliable statements attributed to
the enigmatic *maggid* ("storytelling spiritual teacher," as I
characterize the phlegmatic Galilean). However, later edi-
tors often framed Jesus' remarks to make it seem as if he
opposed standard Jewish practices, *kashrut* prominent
among them. The early Church sought distance from Jews
and portrayed the deceased *maggid* as more of an outsider
to mainstream Judaism than he likely had been. In fact, in
Acts 10, God (via a voice from heaven) dramatically
demonstrates to Peter that from now on the laws of
kashrut have been abolished by Divine decree.

A scholarly, interfaith, academic consensus holds that
Jesus' statement was not at all beyond the spectrum of
Judaism of his time. My own sense is that Jesus did not
oppose *kashrut* in its own right. In fact, in one of the
best-known Gospel passages, Jesus is quoted as having
said:

> Don't imagine that I have come to annul the Law
> [Torah] or the Prophets. . . . I swear to you, before
> the world disappears, not one iota, not one serif, will
> disappear from the Law, until it's all over. Whoever
> ignores one of the most trivial of these regulations,
> and teaches others to do so, will be called trivial in
> Heaven's domain. (Matthew 5:17–19 in *The Five
> Gospels*, Funk, *et al.*, a collection of scholars also
> known as "The Jesus Seminar")

Jesus' message harmonizes with other Jewish voices
from his era: Of course we observe *kashrut*, but what
comes out of our mouths is *equally* important. See, for
example, how the sages in Mishnah *Baba Metzia* 4:10 and
the *Gemarah* (56B) interpret the prohibitions in Exodus
22:21 and Leviticus 25:14 to include an ever-expanding list
of verbal wrongdoing, particularly fraud. Indeed, which,
if any, of the giants of Judaism *didn't* devote considerable
attention to the whole matter of *lashon harah* (evil speech)?

As a rabbi working within the framework of Conservative Judaism, I am both personally observant of *kashrut*
and encourage others to deepen their level of dietary
loyalty to the God of Israel. Like many of my fellow
contributors to this volume, I, too, was raised in a family
unconcerned with these ritual observances and came to
these practices as an adult. I, too, struggle to balance my
concern for *kashrut* with the equally important values of
shalom bayit (peace in the house) and *kavod av v'em*
(honoring father and mother). None of these values
supercede the others. Each has an equal claim on me, no
more or less than the others.

The elevation of *kashrut* (and *Shabbat* observance, for
that matter) as the litmus test of one's Jewish religious
legitimacy concerns me as it raises one set of somewhat
superficial, concrete *mitzvot* over all others. *Shabbat* and
kashrut share the virtues of being public, countable, and
visible. They are the most "in your face" of the *mitzvot*, not
necessarily the deepest. It is much more difficult, if not
impossible, as just two of many possible examples, to
measure how respectfully one may or may not act toward
older people or how much one does or in fact does not
love God. Which *mitzvot* are more important than these, to
name just two?

So, on this issue, I'm with Jesus, and probably Hillel,
the likely source of much of his teaching. I try not to let
my concern about a questionable ingredient that my host

or hostess may have unwittingly included outweigh the hurt and insult that a Kitchen Inquisition would engender. I would rather risk unwittingly eating a carcinogenic non-kosher chemical instead of an equally lethal laboratory brew bearing a *hechsher* if it will help me avoid needlessly embarrassing another person.

On the other hand, when I visit my family of origin and, after twenty-five years, whoever ordered the pizza "forgot" that some of us don't consider pepperoni a suitable topping on the pizza, it's time to invoke Hillel's sterner side: *Im ain ani li, mi li?* ("If I am not for myself, who will be for me?")

Life consists of tension and of dynamic balances, and the mouth is its most public arena and thoroughfare. It is a two-way street, and the traffic in both directions is equally vital. I try to monitor and control the flow in and out. Sometimes I fail, especially around family; sometimes I succeed. We *can* eat our meals across the great paper plate divide and not deride one another's Jewishness. What we say over our bread is *as* important (not more or less) than the *hechsher* on its package.

25

NOT A MISTAKE
Rabbi Shlomo Riskin

(from *Shabbat Shalom: Behalotcha*—June 3, 1999)

I'd like to share a personal story. Some readers may already know from my writings in the past that I was not born into an observant family. Because the yeshiva in my neighborhood was considered far more academically challenging than the local public school, my parents consented to my grandmother's urging that I receive a day-school education. But living in a non-observant home required certain balancing skills. On Friday nights I would join my grandmother for the *Shabbat* meal, and every *Shabbat* lunch I was invited to the home of the principal of our yeshiva, Rabbi Menahem Manes Mandel, who remains a powerful influence in my life.

After returning to my neighborhood of Bedford-Stuyvesant, I would spend a quiet hour with my mother, a kind of quality time when we would both talk about what was closest to us. The latter part of the afternoon I would spend with Saul Berman, the son of a prominent community Rav and my special *Shabbos* friend.

But one particular *Shabbat* while my mother and I were busy talking, there was a knock on the front door. When my mother saw it was my *Shabbos* friend, she hid the cigarette she was holding behind her back.

When my mother came back into the living room, still holding the cigarette, she looked at me and said rather sadly, "I think God made a mistake by putting you and me together. You're religious, and every day becoming even more religious, and I'm not interested in religion at all. Why should God have given me a son like you?"

My response was clear—I really believed what I was saying—that I'm sure that God didn't make a mistake at all. I told her that not only was I religious but I even wanted to become a rabbi. "I think God made you my mother so that I would learn that you have to love everybody, even people who aren't necessarily obser-vant." In retrospect, that attitude more than any other, which I learned from my mother, has been a guiding principle of my life.

26

THE TRIANGULATED RABBI: STUCK BETWEEN THE *BA'AL TESHUVAH* AND THE FAMILY

Rabbi Mordecai B. Twerski

*I*n geometry we learned that the triangle is the most rigid geometric form and is therefore used in architecture to enhance stability in many structures. Examples of this principle are evident in most steel bridges and steel building frames. This concept, however, has some serious negative repercussions in relationships. When families become triangulated, the rigidity locks the members into patterns that cannot be changed without the fear of threatening the stability of the family.

Change takes place in families if we are ready or not. Parents age, children go through adolescence, and the various stages in family life cause the shifting of the former stability until a new and hopefully better equilibrium is established. When a family member, classically a child, becomes intensely religiously involved, the stress that this places on the family system can often be severe. For the contemporary Jewish family, this has become one of the more common yet painful situations that are brought before the rabbi's eyes.

The parents or siblings of the *ba'al teshuvah* (literally, the owner of the process of "returning") will often come to their rabbi seeking guidance. Often the family lays a rather heavy burden upon his shoulders regardless of whether the rabbi has been part of the cause for the religious inspiration or not. Even if the rabbi does not endorse the particular form of religiosity that the new adherent is practicing, the inference the rabbi hears is, "Judaism is ruining our lives." The pre-existing family dynamics are often overlooked. The religious system becomes the perpetrator. If the rabbi had a part in the spiritual renewal of this family member, then the criticism of "how could spirituality be causing so much hurt" gains validity. It brings into question the essential values that the rabbi holds dear for himself and the community.

The corners of this new triangle become the family, the *ba'al teshuvah*, and the rabbi. The primary response for the rabbi can be to shift his role to becoming the bridge for the family members, allowing a new dialogue to replace the pain of the conflict.

The bridge metaphor has some handy parables. In order to build a bridge, an initial evaluation should be made of how great is the gap that needs to be spanned. One would prepare different materials and tools if he is trying to span a stream versus the Grand Canyon. Once the size of the gap has been ascertained, what are the strengths upon which the bridge will be anchored? Are new footings needed to be sunk upon which the supports will rest or are the walls of the sides strong enough to support the new bridge? What would the design of the bridge look like? Does the design need spires from which to hang suspension cables or will building a supporting arch under the roadway suffice?

In using these as guides for the rabbi, the evaluation might begin with the following questions: What was your relationship with this child like before he/she became involved with religion? What were some of the strengths of those earlier experiences? How might those strengths be helpful now? How often are you in contact with him/her? Is the distance a physical one as well as emotional? What happens when you spend real time together? When are you able to share family events? What makes this work and what gets in the way? Who in the family maintains the best communications with him/her? How do they get around the disagreements? What values have carried through into the new religious lifestyle? How have you contributed to the strength of those essential and underlying values? What acknowledgment do you give him/her and yourselves for the strength of those basic truths and values that have always been part of the family system?

It is far better to be a facilitator of communication than to be the pointed pinnacle of the triangulated family. The help that the family needs would be ill-served by the rabbi or religious representative becoming defensive and attacking the concerns of the family members on either side of the dialogue.

27

A ROCK AND
A HARD PLACE
Rabbi Amy Wallk-Katz

I grew up in a kosher home, although my parents did not insist that we eat kosher food outside of the house. It was not until 1978, when I was sixteen years old and studying in Israel, that I decided it was important for me to eat kosher food even outside of my home. I was searching for ways to make my life more Jewish. Through my courses at Hebrew University, I was learning more about Judaism, but I wanted to incorporate more ritual into my daily life.

I was not a veteran of Jewish camps or youth groups. My knowledge of traditional Judaism was very limited and I had no synagogue skills. As a result, going to synagogue more regularly did not appeal to me. *Shabbat* observance was not an option. The more traditional community intimidated me and I did not want to separate myself from my friends at Hebrew University. In contrast, observing the dietary laws all of the time seemed accessible. I knew the laws of *kashrut*, and living in Jerusalem made things especially easy for me.

At the end of my year abroad, I debated how to continue keeping kosher. I consulted with family and friends. Some people were supportive while others were concerned that I was getting too religiously observant, too *frum*. One of my professors, a Conservative rabbi, enabled me to find a balance. I decided that I would eat cooked dairy and vegetarian foods prepared in non-kosher kitchens. This permitted me to accept invitations to friends' homes and to eat cooked dairy and vegetarian foods in non-kosher restaurants.

The challenge of embracing two cultures is great. But so too are the rewards. I enjoy participating in American society and am grateful for the many opportunities that have been afforded me. At the same time, I am proud to be separate and committed to clinging to Jewish traditions.

Even when I applied to rabbinical school nearly a decade later, I did not change my *kashrut* practices. I felt as though I had a perfect balance. I could at once observe the Torah's commandments and fully participate in the activities around me. While I understood that some people believe that the purpose of *kashrut* is to limit one's social interactions, I rejected that interpretation. I purposefully chose to keep kosher in such a way that I could continue socializing with friends and family who do not share my religious commitments.

I had no idea how my *kashrut* practice would complicate my life. By taking such a liberal stance, I assumed that my religious commitments would not interfere with my personal relationships. Nor would they dictate with whom I would associate. I assumed that most people would accept my compromises and respect my religious commitments. My assumptions were wrong.

What began as a personal expression of my Judaism has become a force of divisiveness and alienation. Some friends and family who do not keep a kosher kitchen have a difficult time knowing what to do with me. They become offended when I explain that I cannot eat meat—even kosher meat—in their homes. It is very difficult for these people to understand why I will eat some foods, but not others, in their homes. They become irritated when I do not allow them to bring cooked foods into my home. They somehow think I am saying their food isn't good enough for me.

Sometimes I, too, get irritated and respond with anger and annoyance. Other times, I understand their feelings because I have a brother who will never eat in my home. Even though I keep kosher, I don't keep kosher enough. Often, I interpret my brother's choice not to eat in my home as his rejection of me and my Judaism. Rather than recognizing my brother's decision as his personal choice, I feel insulted and alienated. I become the person feeling "not good enough."

Where does all this leave me today? Does my *kashrut* practice still make sense to me? How do I continue a religious practice that alienates some friends and makes me feel alienated by others?

My challenge is to be attuned to how other people feel when I won't eat meat in their houses. I know how I feel when my brother will not eat in mine. Similarly, when my brother chooses not to eat in my home, I can't allow myself to get angry with him. I have to remind myself that his interpretation of religious duty is different than mine.

It isn't always so easy to remember this, especially when feeling defensive or vulnerable. But that's the challenge.

Part IV

Conclusion

28

TOP TEN THINGS TO DO IF YOU'RE MORE OBSERVANT THAN YOUR FAMILY
(for *Ba'alei Teshuvah*)

1. Buy a set of plates for your parents. Don't wait around for your family to go shopping. They're overwhelmed by all this *kashrut* and you can make it so much easier for them if you give them a set of plates, silverware, a couple pots and pans, and some placemats. Arrive bearing gifts. (Bring aluminum foil.) Then find a place in the kitchen (or the garage) to store your kosherware. If you visit your family often, the kosherware will soon replace the Chef-Boy-R-Dee in the cupboard, but don't push it.
2. Take your parents on a field trip to the grocery store. Show them the different *hechshers* on the food. Really walk the aisles. It will be very reassuring for them.
3. Never promise you will not become more observant than you are that particular day.

4. Use labels in your house. Label the cupboards, the drawers, the sink, and so on. Use all types of audio-visual aids, including charts that tell which of your favorite foods are still okay.

5. Travel with food. Arrive at their door with a box of Entenmann's donuts and some apple juice. Allow your family to enjoy your visit without the anxiety of "what will I feed him?" Grocery stores are open all night; no excuses.

6. There are people, even rabbis, who will tell you to separate yourself from your family. Don't listen to them. You can live an observant life without alienating the people who love you. Your observance is built on the bedrock of Judaism. You do not need to ruin loving relationships to create a meaningful, observant life.

7. Find a way. Don't let *kashrut* stand between you and your attendance at family events. It's more important to be there than to eat there.

8. You've changed; they haven't. You have an obligation to explain what you're doing and why. And while you're explaining, tell them how much you appreciate what they *have* given you. Be sensitive to the fact that you are usurping the role of teacher in the family dynamic. And although it's possible that your observance will inspire your family to pursue more knowledge of Judaism, don't count on it.

9. Wake up early on Sunday so that you can get everything done, including a visit to your family. Reassure them that your *Shabbat* observance does not mean that you no longer will have time to spend with them.

10. Have a sense of humor.

29

TOP TEN THINGS TO DO
IF SOMEONE IN
YOUR FAMILY BECOMES
OBSERVANT

1. Ask questions. Don't accuse, don't point out what seem to be glaring inconsistencies, just ask. You don't need to have a major discussion about, for example, "faux" food—soy pepperoni pizza or non-dairy "whipped cream" desserts. And avoid discussions about wasted electricity on *Shabbat* (timers, ovens left on, and so on). But ask, in a nice tone of voice, how you can make the person comfortable.
2. *Kashrut* is not rocket science. It seems confusing at first and you'll make mistakes, but that's okay. Invest in aluminum foil. Learn to double wrap.
3. If possible, serve food, such as cookies or crackers, in the original packaging. That way, someone can casually check the *hechsher*. It lessens the amount of discussion about food and *kashrut*. Also, don't dress

the salad. Set the salad dressing bottles on the table.
Some salad dressings, even ones that don't appear to
contain dairy products, may be okay for a dairy meal
but not for a meat meal.

4. Eggs are *parve*, neither meat nor milk. (It's not intui-
tive. It seems as though eggs would certainly be a
dairy product, but they're not.) Therefore, eggs can be
used at any type of meal.

5. If you can afford it, order kosher deli trays and use
kosher caterers. Try a kosher resort or a kosher cruise.

6. If your son or daughter has become observant, accept
the fact that your child has changed. It does not mean
that you should have or could have done anything
differently. Be prepared for the role reversal that
occurs when your child becomes your teacher in a
non-credit course called *Kashrut 101*.

7. Assume that observance is a moving target. Just when
you think you understand what the newly observant
person expects, he or she will change the rules. There
is no standard "Orthodox." Different Orthodox communities have different customs, so don't even bother
comparing what Freida's cousin does with what your
son expects.

8. Develop different family traditions. Even though you've
always gone to Aunt Maxine's house for Rosh Hasha-
nah, you might need to change that family custom.
And don't be shocked if you find yourself adopting
some Jewish rituals. Judaism is not an all-or-nothing
prospect.

9. Don't mess with Passover. Passover is a time when
newly observant people get a little nervous (an un-
derstatement), so don't even think about trying to do
Passover.

10. Have a sense of humor.

CONTRIBUTORS

Marsha Arons is a freelance writer. Her work has appeared in *Reader's Digest, Good Housekeeping, Redbook, Woman's Day* and *Woman's World,* as well as many Jewish publications. Arons is also a regular contributing author to the *Chicken Soup for the Soul* series. Her story, "One White Gardenia," is the first story in *Chicken Soup for the Woman's Soul* and remains one of the most popular and best-loved stories in the collection. In addition, Arons does promotional/marketing work and directs and produces promotional videos. Currently, Arons' projects include a collection of short stories as well as a novel for teenagers. Arons is married and the mother of four daughters. She lives in Skokie, Illinois, and can be reached through her e-mail address: *ra8737@aol.com.*

Brent Baer is the president of The Baer Essentials Company, a training and consulting firm specializing in communication, presentation, and professional development skills. He coaches a variety of clients, ranging from rabbis to CEOs to lawyers. Brent left the Washington, D.C., area in 1991, where he was named as Dale Carnegie Training's top worldwide revenue producer, to take a six-week "leave of absence" from his job to learn more about his Jewish roots. Six weeks quickly "expanded" into two years of learning Talmud, Jewish law, and ethics in yeshivas in Monsey, New York, and Jerusalem. Brent and his wife, Mali, live in the New York City area and continue to be involved as active members of their Torah observant community. His e-mail is *speak100@aol.com*.

After graduating from Swarthmore College, **Yosef Branse** wrote and edited copy at *TV Guide Magazine*. A visit to Israel sparked the process of becoming an observant Jew. He has lived in Israel since 1979, currently residing in Rechasim with his wife, Devora, and five children. He works as a systems librarian at the University of Haifa Library.

Rabbi Robert Dobrusin is a graduate of Brandeis University and the Rabbinical School of the Jewish Theological Seminary. He was ordained in 1982. Rabbi Dobrusin has served as rabbi of Beth Israel Congregation in Ann Arbor, Michigan, since 1988. He and his wife, Ellen, have two children, Avi and Michal. The Dobrusins also share their home with a big, brown dog, Silky.

Jim Estin, who was raised in Boulder, Colorado, now works at the Child Psychiatry clinic at the University of Iowa Health Center. He is concurrently working on his doctorate in clinical social work. Jim spent fifteen years involved with the Denver Reconstructionist Jewish community and a *havurah* before he and his wife, Ann, and their two daughters moved to Iowa City.

Singer/songwriter **Peter Himmelman** lives in California with his wife and four children. His first solo album, *This Father's Day*, was released in 1986. Himmelman's popular CDs include *My Best Friend Is a Salamander, From Strength to Strength, Flown This Acid World, The Himmelvaults-Vol. I,* and *Love Thinketh No Evil*. Peter's mother, **Beverly Fink,** has four children and thirteen grandchildren—all wonderful, all Jewish, not all kosher. She got her first teaching job when she was forty years old, the same week Peter had his bar mitzvah. She stayed in education until her retirement in 1987. Beverly was married to Peter's father for nearly thirty-two years, until his death. She remarried thirteen years ago.

Millicent Friedman is a retired teacher of the speech and language handicapped. She received her bachelor's and master's degrees at Hunter College. She has eleven grandchildren for whom she cannot claim responsibility, but she wishes to claim her inalienable right as a grandmother to boast about them.

Lynn Geller is a wife, mother of two girls, and Senior Project Manager for IBM. Lynn grew up in Denver, Colorado, in a Conservative Jewish home. Lynn is the youngest of five children, three of whom live Orthodox Jewish lives. Lynn continues to follow the Conservative movement's tenets, belonging to the Hebrew Educational Alliance in Denver. Lynn also serves on the board for the Colorado Agency for Jewish Education (CAJE).

Gary Kornfeld is a real estate broker in Boulder, Colorado. He is vice president of Kehilath Aish Kodesh, a budding Torah-observant community. Despite a short-lived attempt at "feeding" the Boulder community with his kosher restaurant, Gary Kornfeld, along with his wife,

Deb, and their daughter, Chava, remain committed to the enhancement of Yiddishkeit and community in Boulder.

Rabbi Joel Lehrfield was ordained by the Hebrew Theological College in Skokie, Illinois, and received both his M.A. and Ph.D. from the University of Chicago. Additional talmudic studies took place during a period of study in Jerusalem. In addition, Rabbi Lehrfield has spent six years of post-doctoral training as a therapist. Rabbi Lehrfield, who has been on the faculty of Loyola University, De Paul University, Mundelein College, and the Hebrew University of Jerusalem, has also held numerous positions in the rabbinic community as well as in the counseling field. He has been the rabbi of Lincolnwood Jewish Congregation in Lincolnwood, Illinois, since its inception in 1958.

Joan S. Levine, a Colorado native and the granddaughter of a rabbi, is a semi-retired schoolteacher. She and her second husband, Arnie, have six children between them. The family includes two interfaith marriages, an Orthodox union, and three unmarried children.

Alan Perlman, an internal medicine physician, served as Medical Director of Primary Care at Andrews Air Force Base in Maryland. In the spring of 2001, he began a fellowship in Nephrology at the Washington Hospital Center in Washington, D.C. Perlman is originally from Phoenix, Arizona.

Alex S. Polonsky is an attorney at a major law firm in Washington, D.C., practicing nuclear and environmental law. He lives with his family in Silver Spring, Maryland.

Rabbi Shlomo Porter is the director of the Etz Chaim Center for Jewish Studies in Baltimore, Maryland. He has been involved in Jewish outreach since 1974 and is currently the president of the Association of Jewish Outreach Professionals. Rabbi Porter is a graduate of the Ner Israel Rabbinical College in Baltimore, Maryland. His and his wife, Shoshana, have five children. He can be reached at *etzchaim@flash.net* or 410-764-1553.

Rabbi Shlomo Riskin received his ordination from Rabbi Joseph B. Soloveitchik in 1963. From 1963 until 1977, Rabbi Riskin taught Bible and Talmud at Yeshiva University. In 1982, Rabbi Riskin was awarded his doctorate from New York University. As a young rabbinical graduate, Rabbi Riskin founded the Lincoln Square Synagogue in Manhattan, and he later founded the Ohr Torah High Schools for young men and women. In 1983, Rabbi Riskin left New York to become the rabbi of the City of Efrat in Israel, where he now lives with his four married children and nine grandchildren. A prolific author, Rabbi Riskin has a regular weekly column on the biblical portion-of-the-week that appears in the *Jerusalem Post* and throughout the world.

Naomi Rothberg, who had a completely secular upbringing, is a law book editor. In the last five years or so she and her husband, Meyer, have become members of the Woodstock (N.Y.) Jewish Congregation, which is unaffiliated but basically Reconstructionist. It is the first congregation membership for them or anyone in their immediate families and, while no more "religious" than ever, both have come to enjoy a sense of connectedness with Jewish community.

Elizabeth Sandler is a retired marriage and family therapist who lives on the West Coast. She and her husband have three children and seven grandchildren.

In 1962, **Rabbi Zalman Schacter-Shalomi** founded the P'nai Or Religious Fellowship, now called ALEPH: The Alliance for Jewish Renewal. In 1990, Reb Zalman was a participant in the historic meeting between the Dalai Lama and eight Jewish leaders, a meeting described in Roger Kamenetz's book, *The Jew in the Lotus*. Reb Zalman's most recent book is *From Aging to Sage-ing: A Profound New Vision of Growing Older*. Reb Zalman currently holds the World Wisdom chair at Naropa Institute in Boulder, Colorado.

Shortly after **Robert Schreibman** entered Dartmouth College in 1953, he discovered that the college did not have a Hillel and that there were no synagogues nearby. Committed to observing the High Holidays, Schreibman, along with some Jewish friends, conducted his first High Holiday service in the college's congregational chapel. Schreibman later graduated from Hebrew Union College with honors, including the Leopold Michels Prize in Hebrew and the Stephen S. Wise Memorial Prize for Meritorious Scholar. Schreibman first served communities in Annapolis, Maryland, and New City, New York. In 1975, Rabbi Schreibman took the pulpit at Temple Jeremiah, a Reform temple in Northbrook, Illinois. For twenty-five years, until his retirement in 2000, Rabbi Schreibman was a leader in the North Shore Jewish community as well as at Temple Jeremiah. Rabbi Schreibman has three grown children.

Rita Schwartz Singer lives in Denver, Colorado, with her family. She coordinates special education programs at the Colorado Agency for Jewish Education.

Allen Selis was ordained at the Jewish Theological Seminary of America in New York. He has served as rabbi at Congregation Bonai Shalom of Boulder, Colorado, and Congregation B'nai Israel in Rockville, Maryland.

Rhonda Slater works for Synagogue 2000 at the University of Judaism in Los Angeles. She and her husband, Mark, are the parents of three sons.

Michael Stein, who was born in 1960, has been married to his wife, Rachel, since 1987, and they have four children. He started observing *Shabbat* and *kashrut* shortly after college, during a six-year period when he lived in Israel. While Michael and his family now live in Skokie, Illinois, they all hold dual Israel-American citizenship and visit Israel regularly. At work, he is a banker specializing in commercial real estate lending. (Editor's Note: Michael Stein is Linda Loewenstein's brother.)

Born and raised in Denver, Colorado, **Rabbi Mordecai Twerski** attended the Telshe Rabbinical Seminary in Cleveland, Ohio, and received his Doctor of Divinity from Yeshiva M'Kor Chaim in Brooklyn, New York. In 1982, after practicing accounting in New York for ten years, Rabbi Twerski moved to Denver to take over the leadership of the Talmudic Research Institute. The Talmudic Research Institute was founded in 1970 by Rabbi B.C. Shloime Twerski, Rabbi Mordecai Twerski's father. It is a community composed of Jews from every background, some of whom have come through the turbulence of many spiritual journeys. Rabbi Mordecai Twerski is heir to centuries of Chasidic spirituality, in direct linkage for ten generations back to Rabbi Israel Baal Shem Tov, the founder of the Chasidic movement in eighteenth-century Russia.

Rabbi Amy Wallk Katz was ordained at the Jewish Theological Seminary of America. She is the adult learning coordinator of the Central Agency for Jewish Education in Overland Park, Kansas, and is writing her dissertation on the teaching of prayer in supplementary school settings.

Rabbi Doug Weber was ordained at HUC-JIR at its New York City campus in 1982. Among his post-ordination training credentials is a certificate from Case Western Reserve University School of Medicine, Department of Psychiatry Pastoral Counseling program. Before becoming rabbi of Congregation Bonai Shalom in Boulder, Colorado, Rabbi Weber served congregations and chaplaincies in Virginia, Ohio, and Maine. He and his wife, Jessica, are the parents of three teenage children and are the authors of *The Jewish Baby Handbook: A Guide for Expectant Parents* (Behrman House, 1991).

INDEX

Linda Loewenstein was born and raised in Chicago, in an assimilated Jewish family with two brothers and the annual Christmas tree. In 1972, Loewenstein married her husband, Mark, the child of German Holocaust refugees. Several years later, Loewenstein's youngest brother became observant, shocking and disappointing their parents. Thus began Loewenstein's journey into the heart of families coping with diverse religious observance. For twenty years, Loewenstein was a professional journalist. Loewenstein and her husband now live in Boulder, Colorado, where she is the director of the Boulder Jewish Community Center. They are the parents of three children.